MW00622868

The Field Guide to
GLOBAL
PAYMENTS

SOPHIA GOLDBERG

The Field Guide to Global Payments by Sophia Goldberg
Published by Sophia Goldberg
Sponsored by Modern Treasury & Lithic

Cover art by Mark Wagner; cover design by Asia Bizior
Edited by Gregory Brown

ISBN: 978-0-578-29526-8 (print)

Printed in USA
First Edition

Contents

Introduction

Five years ago, when I started working in the payments industry, a book like this didn't exist. I sure wish it had. With *The Field Guide to Global Payments*, I set out to write the book I could have used then. I'm hoping it's the book you can use now.

This is by no means a picture of the entire industry, which is complex and quickly changing. Instead, it's meant to be a survey course in payments. Together we'll move through different elements of the industry, seeking to understand terminology, the working mechanics of various payment systems, and how different business models have key payments considerations. I'm hoping this knowledge is relevant to merchants, folks at payments companies, and those who would just like to better understand the industry.

Several books on payments exist already, and while they're a great introduction, most lag behind on two fronts. First, they are very United States-centered. Secondly, they tend to focus overly on credit card transactions. The payments landscape outside the United States and beyond credit cards is huge. In fact, it's growing daily. I think global, multi-dimensional payment literacy is crucial.

WHO IS THIS BOOK MEANT TO BE FOR?

Well, it's for anyone who is either interested in payments or in a role that touches payments – that could be an accounting team who interacts with payments, someone starting a job within a payments company or payments team, or executives who want to learn more about the mechanics of where much of their revenue *literally* comes from.

The payments industry is daunting but crucial. It underpins the entire modern globalized economy. It's hard for someone starting off to know what they don't know. The great thing about being a beginner, though, is the space to grow and learn that it provides. This book will give you a high-level understanding of the different aspects of payments – this is not an encyclopedia but a field guide, a reference to understand payments as a whole.

Many companies see payments as a cost center. I'm clearly biased as a payments professional, but in the twenty-first century payments should no longer be an afterthought for any organization.

There are many individuals with more tenure and expertise in payments than me – I have learned a ton from several of them during my time in the industry, and in turn have also taken on training new entrants. The diversity of my experiences in the field has given me a deep understanding of payments, globally. I also remain intensely curious about this complex, world-influencing system that runs in the background of all our lives. The more I've learned, the more compelled I've become to share both my knowledge and my continued curiosity with those who are curious about the field and don't know where to begin.

When I was starting out, there were only two books to turn to: *Payments Systems in the U.S.* and now more recently *Anatomy of a Swipe*. I consider both essential reading, but I still believe there's a gap to be filled. *Payments Systems in the U.S.* is written *for* payments professionals. I still highly recommend it, but the book isn't an approachable first foray into the industry for many. It's also narrow in its focus, exclusively covering the United States, much like *Anatomy of a Swipe* is focused only on card transactions, which represent a portion of the current global payments landscape.

I began to ask, "can I fill the gap here?" I know enough to know I don't know everything, but what I do know I know will be valuable to many of you out there. I spoke to colleagues, merchants, and other friends in the fintech and payments spaces. I asked what they would want included and what they would like a book like this to look like if they were, for example, giving it to new starters on their teams. I also wanted it to be readable and approachable for the general public.

With the financialization of the world, for many organizations payments has moved from a begrudging cost center into a core part of their strategies. Isn't it time to better understand how those strategies really function and how they affect both business and consumers at each end?

A QUICK HISTORY OF PAYMENTS

As humans moved past bartering, we cycled through many different forms of currency. From cattle, to cowrie shells, to gold, to central bank regulated fiat currencies, societies have decided what would represent agreed upon value since the beginning of time. Money is, simply put, anything that represents relative value: a store of value, unit of account, and medium of exchange.

Those identified mediums of exchange have rapidly changed over the past decades. Under the gold standard, or any resource-backed currency, money was an abstract IOU – bills and coins (money) functioned as a promise that the central bank could exchange for "real money" (reserves) like gold and silver. One obvious problem with that system: there could only be as much money in circulation as the central bank had in reserves (say, gold). Moving all that gold around was also a hassle. During the course of World War One and World War Two, the British lost more than 4.5 million pounds of reserves to the sea as ships carrying gold and silver to pay suppliers sank. Not so ideal for a monetary system, is it?

In 1931, the United Kingdom abandoned the gold standard. In 1971, the United States followed suit. Coins and paper money became the money itself, no longer backed by gold and silver reserves, and that system remains in place today. Central banks can increase or decrease the monetary supply as they so choose, though they're heavily regulated (I will spare you a recollection of my monetary economics graduate school courses). This also means that the confidence individuals have in fiat money can quickly degrade with economic and political instability – today we see some of this sentiment being directed towards crypto-currencies like Bitcoin.

But what about the mechanisms of moving that money? Daily check clearing began in the 1770s, when clerks from different banks met at the Five Bells tavern in London to exchange their checks. In 1871, Western Union began money transfers. Since then, the pace of innovation has only increased. Online commerce kicked off in the early 1990s. The earliest ecommerce transaction is widely believed to be for a Pizza Hut pizza in 1994, in Santa Cruz, California. Now online sales are the most common way to order a pizza – in 2020, ecommerce ordering accounted for 75 percent of Dominos orders.

Then, in 1994, Jeff Bezos decided books would be a great online purchase. Over the course of the next two decades, books expanded into every category as Amazon became the way for American consumers to buy anything from anywhere, and quickly.

Clippings of rare plants, used sneakers, drop-shipping, direct-to-consumer luggage. We now have the ability to securely pay for almost anything online, at any time.

But how do these transactions really work? What makes an online payment tick, so to speak? The "how" behind this commerce is what this book delves into as the mechanisms of payments have become key to the backbone of our ever-globalized world.

OUR PAYMENTS ROAD MAP

Learning the vocabulary is half the battle of understanding any new industry. What is an acquirer? A pull transaction? And what does a correspondent bank really do? You may know those answers already, but, if you don't, you're in the right place to learn.

In Section One, I'll cover the most basic terms and concepts of payments and dive deep into cards.

In Section Two, I'll focus on non-card payments, breaking this realm down into a handy taxonomy that will help you understand most payment methods you encounter. We'll cover bank-based methods, installments and delayed payments, cash-based methods, and digital wallets. For each method, I'll try to give you an overview of how it works, the path of a payment, some historical context, geographic nuances, and at least one illustrative example.

My hope is that by presenting the types of payment methods you're more easily able to recognize and understand any future methods you see. Yes, there are methods that deviate from this, and with the pace of innovation in payments and fintech globally I wouldn't be surprised if new methods crop up before this book is published.

By this point, we'll have a deep working knowledge of the types of payments one might encounter and the various ways they might come up. But our payments literacy shouldn't stop there.

In Section Three, compliance and fraud are covered. They're important areas to understand. I'm no expert in regulation, fraud, or credit risk, but Matt Janiga, General Counsel of Lithic, contributed a section on the regulatory landscape of payment for an in-depth expert's view.

That covers what payments are and how they work. But what about *where* payments occur and *how* they're applied? In Section Four, I'll discuss three business models where payments should be a key consideration, not an afterthought: subscriptions, marketplaces, and a special B2B chapter authored by my friends at Modern Treasury.

Think of this book as a jumping off point into payments, if you will. The information covered should give you solid mental scaffolding to more easily move deeper into your payments journey. With hope, it will also guide your future learning.

Innovation often starts from a strong foundation of knowledge. Let's open our field guides and begin.

Section One – Cards

Card payments are second nature to many of us at this point. Since we already have an understanding of those transactions, let's start our payments journey there. I also think the flow of a credit card payment brings up core key concepts, so starting here lets us dig into a broad set of topics. Later on I'll also use this section to introduce and go over some aspects that are more specific to card payments, like cross-border acquiring.

A QUICK HISTORY OF CARDS

Considering the growing global prevalence of credit cards, let's start with some history to see how we've reached swipe saturation in such a short time.

One of the earliest noted uses of the term "credit card" dates all the way back to 1887. In his utopian novel *Looking Backward,* Edward Bellamy described the concept of using a card for purchases; he used the term "credit card" eleven times in the novel. In 1946 the first bank card, Charg-It, was introduced by Brooklyn- based banker John Biggins. A user's bill was forwarded to Flatbush National Bank, and the bank settled the amount with the merchant directly and collected the funds from the user's bank account. Only a small number of merchants were supported by the program – those in a specific two-square-block radius – and the card could only be used by those who banked with FNB.

The first credit cards were issued by department stores and oil companies, and the first cards that could be used among broader merchants were created in the 1950s by Diners Club and American Express, though both were still closed loop (we'll define that concept later). The Diners Club card could initially be used at fourteen restaurants in New York initially; within a year that ballooned to three hundred and thirty merchants.

In 1958, Bank of America began licensing the BankAmericard to other banks in other states and countries, creating the open-loop network card payments that dominate the industry to this day. To get its start, Bank of America mailed sixty thousand BankAmericards to residents in Fresno, California in a marketing experiment that came to be known as the "Fresno Drop." In the 1970s, the National BankAmericard Inc., which managed the U.S. card program, and the international arm joined to create Visa.

Visa, closely followed by MasterCard, both created associations of member financial institutions. They created the rules for membership, associated fees, and transaction rules. In return, the card-issuing banks were able to offer consumer lending products in the form of a credit card. Membership was strictly limited to banks and regulated financial institutions – that's why, even today, to be a full-stack acquirer a PSP (payment service provider) must have banking licenses. Initially, many member banks were both Issuers and Acquirers, but with the rise of electronic point-of-sale devices (POS) in the 1980s there was a large drop off of banks acting as acquirers. Changing economics were a key reason – issuing credit cards produced more revenue than the POS fees an acquirer would make.

While it's amazing how much progress payments have made in the intervening decades, it's also astonishing how similar card payments are to their origins.

THE PLAYERS

Now let's cover how a card payment works, and who is involved. The key players in a card transaction have stayed the same for the past seventy years. These are the merchant, cardholder, issuing bank, and acquiring bank. Together, we call this the "four-party model."

The **Merchant** is a company who sells goods or services and wants to accept payments from customers.

A **Cardholder** is the customer attempting to purchase from the merchant. This can be an individual or an entity, in the case of B2B (business-to-business) transactions.

The **Issuing Bank** is the bank that issues a customer's card. The cardholder has a direct relationship with the issuing bank. The issuer is responsible for allowing or denying a transaction, extending credit, and collecting the balance at month's end.

An Acquirer is the merchants' bank partner who processes payments on their behalf and is a licensed member of the card networks. They connect to the card networks and are in the money flow to acquire settled transactions and push those funds to the merchant. An acquirer can be a bank, processor, gateway, or an independent sales organization (ISO). They are members of the card networks and are liable for their merchants' actions and transactions. The acquirer is responsible for four key aspects of payments: authorization, clearing, settlement, and reversals (refunds and chargebacks). We will touch on these in more depth in the next section.

In reality, this four-party model has a fifth player, by many accounts the most influential one: **The Networks**. Think of it this way: if the players in the game are the Issuers, Cardholders, Merchants, and Acquirers, then the network is the board on which the game is played. The network provides infrastructure, the rules for how parties interact, and aggregates funds so not every issuer has to talk to every acquirer.

THE NETWORKS

The card networks, also referred to as schemes or brands, connect acquirers to issuing banks, provide a clearing house function, set the rules of engagement, and determine transaction fees. They provide the rails and rules for card-based payments to occur. The networks play the key role of sitting between issuers and acquirers and acting as the force multiplier that passes transactions between the two, connecting an exponentially larger group of participants in the network's payment ecosystem.

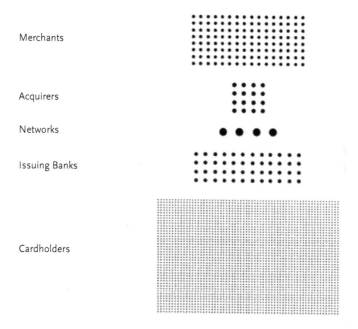

Merchants

Acquirers

Networks

Issuing Banks

Cardholders

While each network sets specific rules that issuers and acquirers need to follow, all networks use the ISO8583 protocol as the communication format. The global card networks are Visa, Mastercard, JCB, American Express, Discover, and China UnionPay.

ISO8583: HOW NETWORKS TALK TO ONE ANOTHER

With so many acquirers and issuing banks it's necessary to have standardized message formats and norms for communicating. Most networks use ISO8583 for real-time authorization. It defines the different message types that can be recognized in that message when transactions are attempted, so all parties know what's going on and the intended actions. Some examples:

MTI 0100: authorization request message from acquirer to issuer in DMS (Dual Message System, we'll define this soon)

MTI 0110: authorization response message from issuer to acquirer with accept/decline in DMS

MTI 0220: financial advice message, from acquirer to issuer, where the advice means that an event took place and must be accepted (SMS)

MTI 0800: is a network management message from acquirer to scheme, i.e. to logon/off a network connection

Let's decode these messages in a bit more depth.

MTI stands for "message type indicator." This four-digit field indicates the function of the message, and each digit communicates specific information. The first digit indicates the version that the MTI is encoded with. The second communicates the purpose of the message (for example, if the second digit is 1, then it's an authorization message). The third digit defines how the message should flow – a 1 means the message is an issuer's response to a previous request. The fourth digit indicates which party in the payment value chain initiated the payment; a 2 means the issuer initiated the message, while a 0 means the acquirer was the source.

Looking at the above examples, you can decode MTI 0100 as:

0 – Version ISO 8583:1987

1 – Authorization message

0 – Request

0 – Initiated by the acquirer

Now we know what some of the major networks are, and a better understanding of the protocol they all use to communicate, let's look at what networks actually do. Open-loop networks such as Visa and MasterCard have a myriad of responsibilities such as:

- Acting as the switch that connects the acquiring and issuing banks in the Network for processing, disputes, refunds, and settlement
- Performing net settlement on behalf of all of those participating banks daily
- Rule setting: creating, maintaining, and enforcing the rules for how banks in the Network interact
- Fee setting: defining interchange rates and scheme fees
- Managing membership in the network, who qualifies and with what criteria
- Dispute arbitration: making rules for disputes to ensure that disagreements on the network are all handled and treated the same way, which also engenders trust from cardholders to use their cards with any merchant.

They pass information and funds between Acquirers and Issuers and define the rules of communication (ISO8583 currently) and fees.

The networks centralize and focus the card-based payments industry. They create the rules of engagement, fees for participation, infrastructure, and rails. They are able to connect thousands of Issuers to hundreds of Acquirers globally. Without them, there would be an overwhelming web of individual connections and flows of funds. Can you imagine if each acquirer needed to collect funds from each issuer? The clearing house function of networks is just as important as the technical connections they facilitate.

FOLLOW A TRANSACTION

What precisely happens when you buy something online? Let's take a credit card transaction, for simplicity's sake, and follow its path through the purchasing system we've so far broken down.

Here's what a transaction, in its most basic breakdown, looks like from a merchant's perspective.

1. Authorization request: Merchant asks, "Can I have $5 from Sophia's account?"
2. Authorization response: Issuer responds, "Yes, sure I'll put $5 on hold for you."
3. Capture/clearing: Merchant, "Great, send me the money."
4. Settlement: Issuer, "Right-o, here's your money." This final agreement sets off a flow of funds from Issuer to Network to Acquiring Bank, who then settles to the merchant.

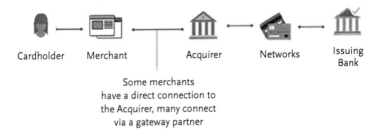

Cardholder   Merchant   Acquirer   Networks   Issuing Bank

Some merchants have a direct connection to the Acquirer, many connect via a gateway partner

Let's illustrate this in more depth, from the merchant perspective.

Value Added Wax is a hypothetical candle merchant. They've built a great product, marketed to and attracted a loyal customer base, run influencer campaigns to generate more interest, and invested heavily in an optimized cart and checkout experience to sell online through their website.

Value Added Wax has done a great job putting their customer scaffolding in place. They currently have one hundred eager shoppers ready to check out with their candles!

On the checkout page, the shopper fills in their payment details. Typically these are the PAN (payment account number, the sixteen digits on their card), the expiry of their card, the CVV (the three or four-digit security code), and their billing address. Pro tip: if you don't send the AVS data (billing address information) in the authorization, you may get an interchange downgrade, which means, in short, that the transaction will cost you more as a merchant. We'll talk about this when we discuss fees later.

Your checkout page can be fully owned and hosted by you as long as you're a PCI-compliant merchant who is allowed to hold and transmit PAN data. If you're not, or you don't want to touch sensitive card data, your payment services provider (PSP) will likely support either drop-in UI components or perhaps an HPP (hosted payment page), both of which may look like your checkout but are actually controlled by your payment provider. These two options give you less control over the user experience and user interface, but also much less data security risk and overhead.

ACRONYM SHAKEOUT: CVV

So often we think of the real meat of a credit card being on its front, where we typically see our name and our card number. Then we're asked for those final few numbers printed on the back before we can finalize a transaction online or over the phone.

The CVV or CVC number is a credit card's security code. The acronyms can be used interchangeably: Visa calls it the CVV, Mastercard the CVC. The three or four-digit number, which is printed on the card, is intended to be used in card-not-present (online) transactions to verify the cardholder. This code *cannot* be stored under PCI standard. Therefore it creates a level of security that ensures the cardholder is physically with the card when making a purchase - it can't be hacked if it's never stored.

ACRONYM SHAKEOUT: PCI

PCI DSS, which stands for Payment Card Industry Data Security Standard and is often abbreviated just as PCI, is the information security standard for any organization that handles card data. It's mandated by the major card networks to standardize protections around the storage and usage of card details and reduce the instances of data breaches of sensitive cardholder data. Before 2006, when PCI DSS was created, each card network had their own rules for how card data needed to be managed.

Sophisticated fraudsters hacking computer networks and stealing payment card data has created a huge problem for the industry, and PCI DSS is a response to this reality. It is a set of requirements that were designed to protect cardholder data on merchant, issuer, and processor systems, and when that data is transmitted between the two. There are three main aspects of PCI DSS:

- Handling the collection and transmission of card details
- Storing this data securely
- Ongoing audits to ensure that the necessary security measures are in place.

Many payment processors will offer integrations that mean a merchant's site never touches card details – either hosted pages a shopper is redirected to, embedded forms, or encrypted fields that the merchant integrates into their checkout. As mentioned above, many payment providers can also offer token vaulting so that a merchant can outsource storing sensitive card details.

Taking on PCI compliance is a large decision – there are more than 1,800 pages of documentation and more than three hundred security controls, alongside yearly audits. There are four levels of PCI, which each have their own requirements that apply to different use cases.

Partnering with a gateway, PSP, or standalone vendor to outsource PCI scope is the decision many merchants make because of this.

Now the customer has filled in their information on the checkout page, and you've sent the request to your PSP. If the customer agrees to let you save their card details – maybe for a subscription you offer or for smoother checkout next time – you will need to *tokenize* the card. This means storing the card details so the cardholder does not have to key them in for a repeat or recurring purchase. We will get into more details on tokenization later as well.

The first question Value Added Wax needs to ask as a merchant is do *they* want to accept this transaction? At the heart of that question is how much risk of fraud they are willing to deal with. They can decide to decline a transaction based on their risk appetite and the data elements of that transaction attempt. Many PSPs offer a built-in risk system. Additionally, there are many third-party options, depending on your use cases and appetite for managing fraud decisioning in-house. Risk-monitoring products give Value Added

Wax a better sense of if the shopper is legitimate and using their own card details.

It's important to take a careful approach to online fraud – merchants want to reduce the number of chargebacks but not to the degree that they stop valid customers from buying. Transaction risk assessment is an art, not a science. It's also a constantly moving target as fraudsters adapt and get sneakier. Frankly, it warrants an entire separate book, so we'll avoid going too deeply into it here.

Let's say their risk system responds, "all good, this looks like a legitimate shopper." Value Added Wax's PSP then sends that transaction to the relevant card network. This shopper has a Visa card, issued by Yoknapatawpha Credit Union. You can tell this from the BIN (first six digits) of the card number, and often just the first number. For example, PANs beginning with the number four are Visa-branded cards.

The networks route the transaction to the relevant Issuing bank (the bank that issued the cardholder the card, our fictional Yoknapatawpha Credit Union here). Here's where the authorization becomes a black box.

While merchants have their own risk appetite for fraud, so does an Issuer. They want to protect their cardholders from fraud and decline transactions that aren't possible – such as those attempted with expired cards or when the customer has an insufficient balance or credit limit. There are lots of refusal reasons, which we'll cover in later sections. For this example, we'll follow the happy path – an authorization!

Yoknapatawpha Credit Union approves the request – this looks like their cardholder shopping, and they have the necessary funds to cover the amount. They place what's called an **authorization hold** on that shopper's account for the amount you requested. Typically an authorization hold is good for seven to thirty days, depending on the issuing bank and the merchant category (i.e., hotels versus retail). Many debit cards hold funds for one to eight days before they release the funds and allow another merchant to use them. You may have seen some merchants even over-authorize the amount they need, like with food delivery, to ensure that if you add tip or the total ends up higher than expected, the merchant has a buffer so they know they can receive the total funds. The networks allow certain merchants (like restaurants, taxis, and parking garages) to instead *adjust* the authorization amount, like to add a tipped amount.

So how does Value Added Wax get the authorized funds? Since the company sells physical goods, it shouldn't set the funds in motion until they're ready to ship the candle. For digital goods, like streaming or digital downloads, you could request funds immediately. This request to set the funds flow in motion is known as **clearing or capture.**

Value Added Wax puts the candles in the mail to the customer. Then they send a request to their PSP to capture the funds that were approved. The PSP sends the capture to the networks – this is generally a batch file sent out a few times a day, though each network has their own cutoff times and ways they like to receive the "capture file."

Clearing is a key function of the networks and the value they add to the card ecosystem. Can you imagine how hard it would be for each merchant to collect funds from the banks of all their shoppers? Or even if every acquirer was to do so?

SETTLEMENT: THE FINAL DESTINATION FOR FUNDS

Settlement is the process through which funds flow to the merchant from the customer's account. In the case of card transactions, the funds flow from the issuer through the network, the acquirer, and then to the merchant. Outside of card networks, funds can flow from the payment method to the merchant – sometimes directly or sometimes through an acquirer.

For card payments, when there is a successful authorization call, a merchant still has to send the capture or clearing request to set the flow of funds in motion. The merchant's acquirer sends that request to the card networks, who act as the clearing house. They go out and collect funds from the individual issuers, bundle them together, and settle the fund to acquirers in a batch.

Merchants are usually **net** settled, meaning the acquirer deducts all relevant fees. Some processors may **gross** settle, where the merchant needs to pay an invoice at month's end for the fees incurred. In reality, many payments providers have a mix of both; they use net settlement for scheme, interchange, and processing fees, but other services like tokenization or risk are assessed at month's end (we'll learn more about these distinctions in the Fees chapter).

But how long does this take? Unfortunately there is pretty wide variance depending on geography and form of payment. From a merchant perspective, it's really important that you know how long the **settlement delay** is for any form of payment that you're going to accept to account for cash-flow concerns.

In the U.S., this process can take two to three days for Visa and MasterCard, but five days for American Express. This is one example where there is *huge* international variability. For example, in Brazil, the settlement delay is thirty days! It's common in some markets for acquirers to offer their merchants a way to receive the funds faster – functionally a secured loan for faster settlement.

For instance, waiting thirty days for a settlement would pose huge cash-flow problems Value Added Wax (and for most merchants). In Brazil, banks offer a solution called acceleration or advancement. Put simply, it's an advance of funds where a merchant pays a percentage markup interest rate to receive funds early – the rate is set by the banks and central bank in Brazil. It's similar to other types of factoring where a company sells their accounts receivable to a third party – but here the buyer is the bank who knows that these funds will come in. There's not a large risk of non-payment for transactions that have already been authorized. Additionally, due to the popularity of installments in Brazil, acceleration also allows a merchant to settle the total or larger partial amount immediately rather than wait twelve months for the customer to complete their installment payments.

Here we've covered a few subjects quickly through our Value Added Wax example. But we also know that not every transaction flows happily to a successful end. What happens when a decline is issued instead of an authorization?

A lot more than you might think.

DECLINES

First, it's important to understand how common declines are before we dive into what happens and how they actually work. Of those one hundred shoppers checking out at Value Added Wax, maybe eighty-five will get approvals. This is what's known as the **authorization rate** or "auth rate." In this example, the auth rate is 85 percent, but Value Added Wax believe they can do better.

Conversion is a term that gets used a lot in payments, but it can mean many things. There's cart conversion: the number of shoppers who add items to their cart versus followed through into sales. Then there are those who click a payment form and never complete the order at the buy button. Checkout optimization can help with that one.

Likewise, there can be many reasons sales don't convert, from a buyer reversing course (less in Value Added Wax's control) to a clunky checkout system (highly solvable). In terms of core payments, though, I think authorization rate is best thought about in a black and white way: the percentage of shoppers successfully paying when they click the "buy" button after entering payment credentials. Those fifteen failed sales could have fallen off due to technical errors, internet outages, page inactivity (down time), issuer refusals, fat-fingering the wrong card number in, insufficient funds, a stolen card, an expired card, a billing address that doesn't match, or a slew of other reasons.

Value Added Wax's marketing, product, and sales teams have put a lot of good work and time into getting customers to buy its product. They want as many successful transactions as possible. They're happy about the eighty-five successes, but what about those fifteen declines! They've worked to drive those purchasers towards their product! As a merchant, what can they do about these declines?

It's important to realize that having some declines is a good thing: you're catching bad actors (fraud) or a shopper using an old or canceled card. No merchant gets an authorization on 100 percent of their attempted payments. However, *false* declines – those where the shopper is legitimate and using their own, legitimate payment credentials – led to $331 billion in lost revenue in 2018, according to a study by 451 Research. Perhaps even more painful is the fact that 40 percent of those shoppers won't return after the initial false decline.

Later we'll cover fraud and risk rules in more depth. For the purposes of this section, we'll look at declines on transactions that the merchant deems legitimate.

Decline rates vary widely by country, payment type, merchant type, and then among individual merchants. There's no great benchmark that provides actionable insight as declines can be ambiguous and nuanced. Merchants do, however, have a lot of agency in improving decline rates. Overall, in-store (POS) transactions tend to have very low decline rates, while ecommerce transactions can have 5 to 10 percent decline rates. Note that the prevalence of declines goes up for recurring transactions, like a subscription payment, or for cross-border transactions. High-risk merchants, like gambling or escort services (what many dating apps are considered by the card networks!), have even lower benchmark auth rates.

DECLINE REASONS

There are many reasons a payment may fail, and many decline codes that card networks and payment providers send back to the merchant reporting on an unsuccessful transaction. These two-digit alphanumeric codes explain *why* a transaction was declined. Each network has their own decline codes, but many processors and gateways translate and map the declines to their own codes to make it easier for merchants to ingest and build logic around various decline responses. This allows a merchant to decide if and how to retry a transaction.

The most common decline reason for an online transaction is "Do Not Honor," sometimes referred to as DNH. It's as unhelpful as it sounds – a black box refusal reason that doesn't really tell a merchant why the issuer is declining the transition. Many Issuers use DNH in place of other specific refusal reasons like "insufficient funds" (NSF), sending the catch-all rather than specific decline code.

It can mean that the transaction tripped the Issuer's own fraud rules, and they don't trust it, leading to a decline to protect the shopper. In the same way merchants should have fraud checks in place, Issuers do as well. They need to protect their cardholders from fraud and misuse. They may see a cross-border transaction as riskier, or a transaction from a different geographic location than where the cardholder lives. Have you ever taken a trip and had your card declined? It used to be normal to call your card issuer to let them know of an upcoming trip so that your travel charges wouldn't be blocked. While DNH is a widespread decline code, others are used as well. Here's a list of common decline reasons, though it's not exhaustive:

NSF: Insufficient funds, sometimes denoted as NSF, means that the cardholder doesn't have available funds for the authorization amount requested.

Invalid CVV: The three- or four-digit CVV that a customer provided does not match the issuer's records.

AVS Failed: The "Address Verification Service" cross-checks the billing addresses a merchant submits with authorization (provided during checkout by the shopper), and the Issuer says it does not match what they have on file.

Expired Card: The card you've submitted is expired – the shopper should update their credentials, or the merchant can request updated payment details with Account Updater (see the subscriptions chapter).

Fraud: The issuer suspects fraud, either based on their internal risk system or other confirmed fraud on the account.

Closed Account: The account associated with this card has been closed, so it can no longer be used.

Invalid Card Number: While the card may pass a Luhn check (briefly, a Luhn check is a public algorithm used to validate that the sixteen digits entered could be a real card number), the PAN sent for an authorization is not an actual card number.

Authentication Required: The cardholder must perform additional authentication like 3DS or 3DS2, either because the issuer is uncertain of the charge or because of local rules and regulations. We'll cover 3D Secure in the Liability section below.

Not Supported: This card can't be used for this type of transaction. Some cards are not enabled for online transactions. Others do not work for cross-border transactions or in other currencies.

NOT ALL DECLINES ARE EQUAL

Now that we understand a few of the common refusal reasons, what's to be done about them? For instance, can Value Added Wax find a way to sort through and target certain declines to retry transactions so that it's not necessarily losing business?

It's important to note that not all refusal reasons should be treated the same. Remember that a certain number of declines are a good thing as declines help prevent fraud. There's what are called "hard" declines and "soft" declines.

Hard Declines are any refusal due to an invalid card, stolen card, or closed account. With a hard decline, there's not much you can do to retry a transaction to convert it into an authorization. At a high level, hard declines shouldn't be reattempted. It's better to prompt the customer for different payment credentials. A canceled card, for instance, will never be authorized, no matter how many times a merchant re-attempts.

Soft Declines can also be considered "temporary" declines. They can be retried with varying degrees of rescue conversion. Overall, 80 to 90 percent of all declines are considered "soft." These can occur for a few reasons – either technical, financial, or incorrect details. Often, there is nothing "wrong" with a transaction or a card. DNH and NSF, for example, can both lead to authorization. For the latter, the cardholder's balance or limit will change over time, so a well-timed retry authorization could be successful.

There's a lot merchants can do with these declines to convert them to authorizations, though it can require investment to do so well. Immediately reattempting transactions with soft declines across another processor can result in a save rate of 1 to 3 percent, according to RPGC Global Consulting Firm. For merchants at scale, this can equate to significant revenue recovery.

Not every soft decline code is equal, and the ways to rescue those transactions vary widely. For example, if it's a technical error, waiting to retry later could resolve the issue. Here there's no need to change fields or the data sent. For an expired card, a merchant can either reach out to the shopper for them to add a new card, or they can reach out to the relevant Network for updated details. This is called "Account Updater" – I go into more depth in the subscriptions chapter in section four. Insufficient funds, however, can take a lot more logic – a merchant should wait to retry when a customer may have more funding in their account, though that can be complicated to deduce and time. I'll go into some of the nuances and assumptions merchants can use to optimize NSF decline retries in the subscription chapter. 3DS and other forms of additional authentication may also be required – for example many cards in Europe (due to PSD2) and debit cards in Brazil. Retrying with the type of authentication required by the network and issuing bank for the specific card can lead to a successful authorization.

Cardholder messaging is also an important consideration. There's nuance in how much information a merchant may want to provide to the customer in the decline response. If it's a fraudster testing cards you don't want to necessarily tell them the transaction was declined because the CVV didn't match. However, merchants want to increase the likelihood of a successful authorization on the second attempt. For this reason, building logic to provide customers with some guidance can pay off.

Instead of "your transaction was declined, please try again," you can tell them that it's an expired card, or that it can't be used to transact in the presented currency. The latter happens quite a bit when merchants add additional markets without full localization. Not all cards are approved on cross-border acquired transactions, or transactions in another currency. Letting the customer know that's the reason for the decline, rather than leaving them in the dark or wondering if they messed up their card number, can save both buyer and seller time and confusion.

CHARGEBACKS

A chargeback is the term for when a cardholder disputes a transaction. At a high level, it is a customer protection – the issuing banks pull back the funds from the merchant in the case of fraudulent activity or poor service. The shopper receives a provisional credit while the chargeback is pending. They occur under certain circumstances, like a fraudulent or unrecognized charge or undelivered goods/services. The issuer will "charge it back" from the merchant via the acquiring bank, reversing the flow of funds. There are "fraud" chargebacks where the cardholder claims to have not initiated the purchase. There are also "service" chargebacks where the cardholder did initiate the payment, but the goods/services were not fully received, and the merchant is not making a customer "whole" through credits, replacements, or refunds.

Once a chargeback is initiated a merchant cannot refund the transaction to "beat" the chargeback – for this reason it's important for merchant customer support teams to take care with handling customer complaints. A chargeback is more expensive than a refund should the merchant lose the dispute, not only do they lose the funds of the settled transaction, but they incur a chargeback fee. This can range anywhere from a few dollars for the largest merchant to much higher, the Stripe base rate for a chargeback is $15. With some PSPs, the fee can be $35 or higher. Chargebacks also have operational costs; merchants have to build workflows to respond to chargebacks.

A third type of chargeback is a technical chargeback, when the transaction was made in error – not through malicious intent or faulty goods/services. Accidental duplicate charges are an example of this – and a great example of where a strong payments operations and customer support team can refund these disputes before the cardholder initiates a chargeback with their issuer.

Chargebacks can be a major cost for merchants for a few reasons. First is needing to return the initial amount, pay the high fee to their processor for the chargeback process, but also because it is important to decide what to do operationally about chargebacks. Let's run through the options.

The first option is to do nothing at all. Maybe you realize that this is indeed a case of fraud, and the best recourse is to accept the chargeback. It's likely that a good number of chargebacks are actual fraud, but this approach shouldn't be used across every scenario. In an ideal world, to combat future fraud chargebacks, a merchant should learn from these chargebacks and update the fraud monitoring systems accordingly. It's important to reduce the number of "legitimate" chargebacks.

The other option is called defending the chargeback. A merchant can dispute the chargeback within forty-five days by submitting defense materials, and in some cases the chargeback will be reversed. One example of valid defense material is sending proof to the issuer that the charge had already been refunded. Others include correspondence with the customer, a signature from the time of delivery (in the case where the customer claims goods never arrived), or other details about the customer and their purchase. If the issuer agrees that the chargeback is illegitimate the chargeback is reversed and counted as "won" by the merchant. Building out procedures to adequate defend chargebacks takes considerable investment, though many fraud system providers have tooling built in to help a merchant manage these processes.

Each network has their own chargeback monitoring programs, merchants with a high count or value of chargebacks compared to their total volume may get fined. A merchant needs to be careful not just at racking up lost revenue from chargebacks, but also of reaching the thresholds set by the networks. Visa's excessive chargeback program is called the VDMP – Visa Dispute Monitoring Program. They divide the previous month's chargebacks by that month's total Visa transactions. If a merchant has 100 chargebacks and a chargeback ratio of at least 0.9 percent they are added to the program to be monitored. Mastercard has the ECP – Excessive Chargeback Program. The ECP divides the number of chargebacks in a single month by the total number of transactions in the previous month over Mastercard. Their threshold for entering the program is one hundred chargebacks and a ratio above 1.5 percent. In the event that a merchant hits these thresholds, they are notified by their acquirer who may also help them to get fraud levels below the threshold.

TYPES OF CARDS

We've followed the path of a transaction for Value Added Wax and explored the different dimensions of declines, including how the company might shift declines into authorizations.

But what types of cards are customers even using for such transactions?

It's not as simple as it might at first seem. In fact, the card landscape has come a long way since Bank of America mail-bombed Fresno with its BankAmericards back in the day.

There are three main types of cards: credit, debit, and prepaid. Each of these types breaks down into an important array of sub-categories. When it comes to credit cards, there's charge versus credit, and non-revolving versus revolving, for instance. Among debit cards, there's signature versus PIN. Finally, when it comes to prepaid cards, there's reloadable versus non-reloadable. Each also has the distinction of closed- versus open-loop. I'm going to give you a high-level look at each type and its main subcategories below. Then we'll move into a more in-depth treatment of the types of cards Value Added Wax are likely to see.

DEBIT CARDS

Debit cards are ubiquitous. If you have a checking account, you almost definitely have a corresponding debit card. A debit card immediately deducts (debits) funds from the cardholder's checking account when used and prevents users from spending more than their current balance. In the U.S, debit cards are used almost twice as often as credit cards.

Debit can be further identified as either *signature* debit or *PIN* debit.

Signature debit cards get their name from the fact that a customer must sign the receipt during an in-store payment, and a merchant must subsequently authenticate that the signature on the receipt matches the signature on the back of the card. Signature debit transactions clear funds from the cardholder's checking account same-day and are usually processed over Visa or MasterCard's networks.

PIN debit cards, however, are authenticated when the cardholder enters their PIN number on a point-of-sale device. Though the funds are also pulled from the cardholder's checking account, they don't always clear the same day. These transactions are also eligible for cashback. When you buy groceries and ask for $20 cash back, that transaction will be processed as a PIN debit transaction. There are many more PIN debit networks than the signature networks. I'll go into that in more depth below.

CREDIT CARDS

Credit cards, unlike debit cards, are not tied to a checking account. A cardholder has a credit limit for the amount their Issuer will allow them to spend, so rather than checking available balance in an authorization like a debit card, a credit card transaction asks if there is sufficient available credit line remaining for the transaction amount.

When it comes to credit cards, they can generally be categorized by how that credit is accessed. Is it revolving or non-revolving (called a charge card)? What does that mean, though?

The distinction is whether the cardholder must pay off the balance in full at the end of the month. For charge cards, which are non-revolving, the balance is paid off monthly. For revolving credit cards, the balance can be carried over, or *revolved*, and paid over time per the agreed upon terms of the card. If you don't pay the full amount off in a given pay period, that unpaid amount carries over to the next period – usually with interest.

PREPAID CARDS

If you've ever been in a large grocery store in the U.S. you've seen the giant display of gift cards. Among them now are pre-paid gift cards branded as Visa, MasterCard, or other schemes. These can then be used at any merchant, rather than a specific merchant like with a closed-loop gift card. A Visa prepaid card is an example of an open-loop prepaid, while an Amazon prepaid or gift card is closed-loop. We get into these distinctions more soon.

There are two flavors of pre-paid cards: reloadable and non-reloadable. Some of the cards you're able to top up with additional funds. This is an important distinction from a merchant acceptance perspective. Some merchants don't accept prepaid cards at all as they're hard to track for fraud (there are no AVS checks for example). Refunds are often not supported (check). A quick pro tip: the major card networks allow for a merchant or acquiring partner dependent to check in the authorization call if it's reloadable or not.

A subscription merchant may not want to allow non-reloadable cards as they'd be dependent on the customer updating new card details when the funds dwindle. But reloadable may be a-ok for their use cases. This quickly starts to get into the realm of business decisions, and a depth beyond the scope of this book.

Purchases made using a prepaid card pull from a balance stored by the Issuer, rather than a checking account like with a debit card.

GIFT CARDS

Gift cards are as complex to give as gifts as they are to manage for the merchants who offer such programs. Some people consider them the laziest gifts; others think they're the best. I mean, hey, with a gift card, you get to pick what you want! That's all well and good, until you start to think, but, hey, hold on, does that mean they don't care about me enough to find a personal gift that I might really enjoy?

That Catch-22 applies on the merchant acceptance side as well. While there are many pros to having a gift card program, there are also a lot of cons – mainly operational and regulatory. Let's explore some of these considerations.

As a business, the case for offering gift cards is straightforward. They provide liquidity for your business, act as customer acquisition if they're gifted to someone who wasn't already a customer and are a great gift to deepen the loyalty you have with whoever buys them. They're also a phenomenal way for customers to budget or for unbanked individuals without a debit card to purchase your goods and services online. They offer flexibility to consumers and cash flow to merchants. Deloitte estimated that 48 percent of consumers planned to buy a gift card for the 2020 holiday season.[1]

Gift cards can also drive more spending. It's rare that a gift card completely covers a purchase. Often, it's a little under or over. If it's over, you've now driven additional sales volume. If it's under, many customers will abandon the remainder on the card. This is called **Breakage**: unused funds that have been paid in full can be good revenue at scale. There are different accounting rules and local regulations around when partial gift card balance can be moved from liability to revenue on a merchant's balance sheet.

Breakage leads us to the pain points of a gift card program, mainly that they are highly regulated. These customer protections aren't a bad thing, but it means there are more considerations to take in when managing a gift card program. Not all unused funds can be considered breakage and counted as revenue – sometimes the balance must be escheated.

Escheatment is the process of returning abandoned funds from a gift card. In many cases the merchant will not know who holds a gift card. In these cases, the funds are returned to the state in line with unclaimed property laws. Each state has their own escheat law outlining what should happen to unclaimed property – like an expired gift card balance.

Furthermore, there's variance on when a gift card is allowed to expire as well as the amounts that can be deemed abandoned. For example, California doesn't allow gift cards to expire, North Carolina only considers 60 percent of the value abandoned, but New York considers 100 percent of the amount abandoned. Wyoming allows merchants to keep $100 of the expired balance, and the rest must be returned to the state.

In addition to escheatment, some states require that gift cards can be redeemed for cash. Some provisions are for only when the amount remaining is low – typically $5 to $10. As many rules around gift cards are state level, you can see why it can be very hard for a merchant to manage the complexity of gift cards. It makes sense then that many merchants will use a third party to manage their gift card program; these companies handle everything from printing the plastic card to managing the regulatory nuances.

Fraud is also incredibly common with gift cards and mainly comes in two forms: defrauding the holder of a gift card and clearing out their balance and using stolen card details to purchase gift cards.

Some analysts estimate that 10 to 25 percent of fraud attempts in ecommerce are to purchase gift cards with fraudulent card details.[2]

This means that merchants should treat baskets that include gift cards with a higher degree of scrutiny and more targeted fraud decisioning.

Another rampant form of gift card fraud is gift card scams where a fraudster convinces an individual to purchase a gift card or prepaid card to pay off a debt or bill. We won't go into this form of gift card fraud in more depth as there's less a merchant can do to prevent such fraud.

Gift card fraud can also "count double" if a $20 gift card allows a fraudster to turn around and spend $20 in goods. If a chargeback later comes in for that $20 gift card purchase on stolen card details, the merchant is out the $20 gift card purchase and also $20 of goods.

CLOSED VERSUS OPEN LOOP

Two key terms in card payments are open loop and closed loop. This tells you whether a card is eligible to be used at just one merchant or across anywhere that card network is accepted. An "open loop" card is what you likely think of when you think of a card. Funds can be spent at a broad array of merchants and is issued with one of the payment networks like Visa, Mastercard, etc. They can be used anywhere that the affiliated card brand is accepted.

Closed loop cards are the opposite – they are restricted to being used between only with specified merchants. Private label credit cards are an example of a closed loop card: many merchants offer credit cards that can only be used at their store. In return shoppers receive rewards or discounts, and credit terms for repayment of the balance.

Gift cards are also an example – 75 percent of gift cards in the US are closed loop, so a majority of the ones you see in the large grocery store display can only be used with the merchant who issues that gift card. Closed loop payments can have benefits such as better economics – the pricing isn't set by the card networks – and also drive loyalty with customers.

American Express is considered a closed-loop network. But you can use the card wherever AmEx is accepted, right? Right. The above closed/open loop definition applies to *cards*. There's also a definition for networks!

Rather than being a closed loop between shopper & merchant, American Express acts as both Network and Issuer. Discover is also a closed loop network. Unlike Visa and Mastercard, they are the entity that approves and extends credit to cardholders. An open loop card network, like Visa, does not issue cards and instead will partner with financial institutions to manage cardholder relationships, extend credit, and issue cards.

CO-BRANDED CARDS

You may have interacted with co-branded or dual-branded cards. Co-branded cards are a joint card between a consumer brand and a card network. Rather than having the card be issued by an issuing bank like Chase, a large merchant acts as the issuer. Many airlines and large consumer brands like Amazon or Costco have card programs. The large merchant on the co-branded card is responsible for deciding who is approved for a card, their credit limit, and the applicable interest rate for carried balances. The merchant, as issuer, is also liable for any bad debt.

Why would a large merchant want to issue cards? One substantial reason is that they then make all or a portion of the interchange fee associated with the transaction. This allows them to offer sign-up incentives or continued discounts, and especially for low-margin businesses like grocery the additional savings through interchange revenue can be meaningful. Additionally, if the co-branded card is "open loop," then the issuing merchant makes a portion of the interchange from wherever else their cardholder/customer spends. American Express has reported that 70 percent of the spending on the Costco AmEx card is made *outside* of Costco. In addition to revenue, the issuing merchant also gets better data on their customers by seeing where else they like to shop.

Customers are drawn to co-branded cards from brands they're loyal to for the points or discounts, whether that's a large discount off your initial purchase or continued perks and points for future purchases, regardless of where you spend on the card. Airlines co-branded cards often come with an initial large grant of miles up front, miles accrued for every dollar spent, and other perks like a free checked bag or lounge access.

We are now seeing many more companies become Issuers, beyond the large retail merchants and airlines. This is enabled in large part by fintech issuing platforms who have modern tech stacks and services to allow merchants to easily stand up a card issuing program. The benefits for smaller companies to issue cards can be both on the financial services side (it's now easier to create a neobank or credit/debit product for a specific user profile) but also for merchants who have use cases like gig economy platforms and marketplaces.

MULTI-BRANDED CARDS

Dual-branded cards are cards that are branded on multiple networks, and thus can be authorized over multiple networks. "Brand" here means card network brand, unlike the "brand" for co-brand cards being the merchant brand who acts as Issuer of the card. This is a key difference.

For example, 95 percent of Cartes Bancaires cards in France are dual-branded with Visa or Mastercard. This allows cardholders to use their cards outside of France and at a larger number of merchants, as not all accept Cartes Banacaires. The card can be processed over the major network rails associated with the card, like Visa. From the merchant perspective they can also choose which network to process the transaction over. There can be fee or authorization rate difference between the different networks, and so more mature merchants may opt to have a payment provider with connections to both networks and the ability to build routing logic to decide which network to use in real time. Cards in Belgium can also be dual-branded, notably Bancontact (BCMC) cards are dual-branded with the Maestro network.

Debit cards in the U.S. are another example of dual or multi-branded cards. One provision of the Durbin Amendment, a section of the 2010 Dodd-Frank Act after the financial crisis, was that all debit cards issued in the U.S. had to have at least one of the PIN-debit networks. Before debit reform in the U.S. (Durbin), 40 to 50 percent of all debit cards only had one affiliated network. Overall, about 79 percent of Visa debit volume ran on cards with no alternate routing option (no co-brand)[3], and about 50 percent of Visa's debit cards had no second unaffiliated network.[4] The main point to requiring all debit cards to be dual-branded was to foster competition. Merchants can route between networks for various reasons: cost, authorization rate, availability.

Durbin capped interchange fees for debit card transactions charged by large banks, and prohibited network exclusivity. This meant that card issuers had to work with more than one network and ensure that each debit transaction could be processed on at least two unaffiliated networks.

Have you seen that sticker with a ton of logos on an ATM? Those are the local networks in the U.S., sometimes called the PIN debit networks. Historically they require a cardholder to enter their PIN when a transaction is processed over that network. However, for ecommerce these networks are "pinless."

Even if the logo is not printed on the back of a debit card, every debit card issued in the U.S. is affiliated with one of the debit networks, and some cards may have more than one. There are more than a dozen debit networks in the U.S., some examples are Star, NYCE, Pulse, Accel, Shazam. Like with the examples in France and Belgium, transactions with U.S.-issued debit cards can also be optimized for cost or authorization rates. Routing the transaction to the most beneficial network depending on the transaction or merchant preference.

Virtual Cards

As you can gather from the name, a virtual card is just that: virtual. There's no tangible plastic card, rather just the sixteen-digit PAN that can be used for online purchases. Virtual cards are designed for single-use, which has the benefit of protecting the actual card account information in the event of a hack. A fraudster with a stolen virtual card number won't get very far: the cardholder's account details stay safe even if their virtual card PAN is leaked. Some virtual cards also allow the cardholder to add additional controls like spending limits or allow them to be used only with specific merchants.

JUMPING ON THE ISSUING TRAIN

Issuing debit or credit cards is in vogue. The reason being that it can, theoretically, move payments from being a cost center to a profit center for many merchants. This is because interchange fees go to the issuer – credit cards tend to turn some of this revenue into rewards – but there are use cases for non-consumer facing companies to issue cards. For example, if you're an airline and give your flight crew per diems for hotels and food, you could have debit cards that can be topped up and used by your crew. This may reduce some of the expense tracking pain and operational overhead, and the company can make money on the interchange where the crew spends those funds. Sounds like a no brainer, right? Not quite. Creating a card program, though now much easier with the help of companies like Marqeta, Adyen, Lithic, or Stripe, is still a large project to manage.

To illustrate more explicitly: An example of a neo-issuing program is one for a delivery app. The app has hundreds of restaurants, drivers, and customers. The delivery platform has a few options for how to ensure the customer's funds get to the restaurant, issuing their drivers a debit card is one great option. This means that the platform doesn't have to work with each merchant individually on an invoicing process or support an expense process for delivery drivers to be reimbursed for the cost of the order. Instead, the driver's debit card issued by the delivery platform is processed by the restaurant like any other card. From the platform perspective, this allows them to have smooth operations, quickly add new restaurants, and make a portion of the interchange on each transaction. While there are huge operational benefits to issuing debit cards to their delivery team, there is also a great revenue opportunity. Note that the delivery platform would be sharing this interchange with their issuing partner/program manager – this revenue also offsets the costs of such a project for many merchants.

BUSINESS MODELS

There are different models to the business of payments. Not every merchant interacts directly with the acquiring bank that processes their transactions; in fact, most do not. In this section, we'll explore ISOs, Payment Facilitator, and Merchant of Record setups.

INDEPENDENT SALES ORGANIZATION (ISO)

ISOs, or Independent Sales Organizations, are a strategy for acquiring banks to onboard smaller merchants and achieve scale of payments volume – without the operational and sales effort to do so. ISOs serve as an intermediary between a merchant and the acquiring bank and play a crucial role in bringing acquirers more merchants while also acting as their point of contact for customer service. They came to prominence in the 2000s but since have been displaced by other models like payment facilitators (more next) – for example developer-friendly gateways like Stripe and Adyen.

What caused a need for ISOs? Was it just a go to market strategy for acquirers to get more merchant customers?

Not quite. ISOs played a pivotal role in getting merchants onto card processing rails and expanding the card payment ecosystem. Before ISOs entered the scene it was challenging for many businesses to accept card payments. They needed to become an approved merchant with the card networks, partner with a bank, undergo comprehensive applications and underwriting – all of this took time and money. Large merchants had an incentive to make the investment, but small merchants simply didn't have the resources. The ISO model unlocked card acceptance for the very long tail of merchants, aiding the proliferation of card acceptance.

They're not members of card associations like Visa and Mastercard but have partnership with acquiring banks. ISOs are a buffer between the very long tail of small merchants that need payment processing and acquiring banks and are much easier for small merchants to connect to to go live with payments.

Unlike Payment Facilitators, who own the relationship with sub-merchants, many ISOs are not contractually involved with the merchant & acquiring bank. Some ISOs own their portfolio of sub-merchants, while others do not – it depends on their specific contracts. ISOs also don't always assume full sub-merchant risk like Payment Facilitators do, this is also dependent on the contract the ISO has with their sponsor acquiring bank. An ISO that is liable for their merchants' risk is called a wholesale ISO, while one that is not liable is a retail ISO.

ISOs also tend to have less flexibility to how they onboard merchants, often needing to use the acquiring banks' processes for onboarding. PayFacs often are able to create their own sub-merchant applications and underwriting procedures, monitoring, etc. within the guidelines set by their sponsor.

ISOs are not in the flow of funds – settlement is directly from the acquiring bank sponsor to the merchant.

PAYFAC: PAYMENT FACILITATOR

The Payment Facilitator model was pioneered by PayPal and Square in the early 2010s, for ecommerce and point of sale, respectively. Mastercard launched their program in 2010, and Visa in 2011. Like the ISO model, it is a story of one-to-many – but unlike the ISO model the PayFac receives a MID (Merchant ID) from the card networks. You could consider it an evolution of the ISO model where the PayFac owns more of the relationship and responsibility for the sub merchant. They have the direct relationship with merchants, are responsible for onboarding, compliance, and also liable for those merchants' transactions and activity. While an ISO resells merchants to an acquiring bank, the PayFac is an intermediary who sits between the merchant and acquiring bank, maintaining the direct relationship. The PayFac is in the flow of funds and is responsible for settlement to merchants, unlike an ISO, but is not the merchant of record (more on that setup below). The merchant is still who is visible to customers on their card statements.

Finix, a platform which helps any company become a Payment Facilitator, defines PayFac as "a payment facilitator is a specialized merchant that has all the privileges of a payment processor: they can underwrite sub-merchants, process transactions, manage disputes, and make payouts on behalf of sub-merchants. Payment facilitators are essentially mini-payment processors."

A PayFac boards smaller merchants within their systems which allows faster speed to market and scales of economy for payment fees, while the PayFac has the direct relationships with an acquirer rather than each merchant. They act as an "aggregator" of the volume, abstracting away some of the complexity of payments and acquiring relationships from their merchants. Payment Facilitators onboard merchants as their sub-merchants rather than as direct merchants for the Payment Provider, the PayFac facilitates payments for these sub-merchants. This is what allows for much quicker onboarding for the merchants. Note that since PayFac is a MasterCard processing model term, it's called Payment Service Provider for Visa.

The networks have rules governing how they can operate – for example American Express requires merchants that meet a threshold of volume processed over the network to have a direct relationship. Additionally, the payment provider a Payment Facilitator uses must agree to allow them to onboard sub-merchants. The PSP will require the Payment Facilitator to have a process for onboarding and underwriting these sub merchants, ensuring adequate due diligence of sub-merchants. The PSP must register the Payment Facilitator with the Networks and ensure that a comprehensive risk and financial review was done in line with their Third Party Agent Due Diligence risk standards. The PayFac also must only board sub-merchants and process payments for goods & services allowed by that PSP. Every acquirer has a list of goods and services that they will not process for on a Prohibited or Restricted Business list, such as counterfeit and stolen goods, gambling, fireworks, even airlines.

The Payment Facilitator is liable for the actions of their sub-merchants, so careful onboarding and monitoring of transactions is important. Per the Visa Core Operating Rules (§5.3.1.1) a payment facilitator is "liable for all acts, omissions, Cardholder disputes, and other Cardholder customer service-related issues caused by the Payment Facilitators sponsored merchants." Mastercard has a similar provision (§7.8.2 ¶2): "The Payment Facilitator must ensure that each of its sub-merchants complies with the standards applicable to Merchants." For example, the Payment Facilitator is responsible for the PCI compliance of each sub-merchant, often ensured by tokenizing payment details for the sub-merchants.

The PayFac is also responsible for complying with anti-money laundering laws – performing KYC "Know Your Customer" and OFAC (US Office of Foreign Asset Control) checks.

A key requirement of PayFacs is also localization – the acquiring rules from the Networks require local domestic sponsorship and entities. This can allow much wider distribution for the PayFac's merchants who would otherwise need their own local entities to process in each relevant country. Many PayFacs are more than just a payment partner for their sub-merchants, often they're offering other services. For example, a platform for workout studios to manage bookings, like MindBody, and who also facilitates those studios to collect payments on the platform.

MERCHANT OF RECORD (MOR)

A Merchant of Record is an entity that process transactions, they're responsible for processing, reconciliation, managing disputes, and funds. Many brands are their own Merchant of Record – think of this simply as the merchant that a shopper sees on their card statement, though some act as an intermediary like in a marketplace. The MOR is the company who customers recognize, owns or takes possession of the goods or services, books sales as revenue, provides customer service, and handles returns. However, the MOR can also be an entity acting on behalf of a merchant, reselling the goods or services directly to a customer. The MOR is responsible for fulfillment of the good or service and the related risks and liabilities associated with payments processing.

The cardholder believes their relationship with the Platform, not the individual merchant. The Merchant of Record books sales as revenue and has a separate process to compensate third parties for goods, either before or after the transaction. The merchant, or the creator of the goods/services, outsources payments to the Merchant of Record. Many marketplaces are Merchants of Record – such as Etsy, Uber, Airbnb, and Amazon. The shopper knows they are buying from that marketplace, can file a chargeback to request a return from them, but on the back end the MOR is reselling goods and services.

According to Visa, the MOR has three functions. First, they're identified to the cardholder as the entity selling the goods or services. Second, it uses its own name to identify itself to that cardholder, and third provides recourse to the customer when there's a dispute.

51

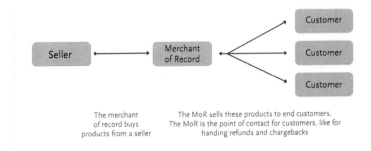

The merchant of record buys products from a seller

The MoR sells these products to end customers. The MoR is the point of contact for customers, like for handing refunds and chargebacks

Some marketplaces are a MOR, while others are a Payment Facilitator. A key way to know the difference is to look at your bank statement – who did you pay? Who do you go to for customer service, a refund, or a dispute?

Both MOR and PayFacs make accepting payments easier for sub-merchants, but they have some key differences. First, a Payment Facilitator acts on a sub-merchant's behalf – each of whom are their own MOR, while the MOR may be the actual merchant or abstract away the core merchant.

To make things more confusing, some entities fall into both categories. PayPal, for example, is the Merchant of Record for small merchants, but for large merchants like Overstock and American Airlines, they are the Payment Facilitator, and that merchant is on the shopper's statement.

ORCHESTRATION

Orchestration platforms are a middleware technology layer for merchants for online payments, sitting between the merchant and multiple providers. They connect to PSPs, fraud engines, non-card payment methods, and other vendors. At first glance they look a lot like a payment gateway; however, I think of the line as being that orchestrators add value *on top of* the technical integrations. Operationally they can serve a similar benefit to merchants as a gateway would – a single token vault, outsourcing ongoing maintenance of integrations, and sometimes a single format for accounting and reconciliation reporting.

Some orchestration platforms add value for merchants by owning the complex routing logic between PSPs for better authorization rates or pricing. Rather than a merchant having to build multiple PSP integration and build then maintain routing logic in house to direct transactions to each PSP, they can outsource this to the platform. The same goes for cost optimization.

ACCEPTANCE ENVIRONMENTS

Card present transactions are any transaction when the cardholder is physically present with their card, like with in-store shopping when the customer swipes or dips their card into a payment terminal. The card must make physical contact with the payment terminal. Manual-key-entry does not count.

Card-not-present (CNP) transactions are any transaction where the physical card isn't presented to the merchant when checking out. But but but, you say. An ecommerce transaction with someone keying in their card details while sitting on their couch is still card present!

Great point. That's how we get the CIT/MIT framework. This further defines CNP transactions into customer-initiated and merchant-initiated. Customer initiated transactions should theoretically include additional data like the CVC code, or additional authentication where relevant, like 3DS. MIT transactions cannot include either, as the merchant is using a tokenized, or stored, credential to process the payment.

Card-not-present transactions existed long before the internet and before the advent of ecommerce, in the form of mail and telephone catalog orders. **MOTO**, which stands for "Mail Order Telephone Order" are seemingly self-explanatory. A shopper would call an agent or mail an order slip to a merchant to complete an order and offer payments over the phone or in writing. This was the first case in card payments where the merchant had no obvious way to validate the identity of the shopper and confirm that it matched the payment details. Fraud is much harder to detect with MOTO payments, and they were then seen as riskier than card-present transactions (fair!). Issuers in turn would not cover the liability of these transactions if a dispute later arose. There's no physical signature or PIN input with a MOTO order to prove that the charge was valid, so the Issuers no longer would own liability for disputes the way they had for in-store transactions.

MOTO payments set the stage for the future of CNP transactions. When ecommerce began many of the same attitudes from MOTO transactions carried over to online payments, especially around fraud and authenticating that the shopper is also the cardholder or authorized to use that card.

SINGLE- VERSUS DUAL-MESSAGE PAYMENTS

Single-message and dual-message transactions are an important concept. But what does this mean? Single message transactions, often abbreviated as SMS, means that a single message is sent to the networks and issuer for a transaction to be completed. Many debit transactions are single message.

If the transaction is authorized, it does not need to be sent for clearing – that process begins immediately.

For dual message (DMS) transactions there are, you guessed it, dual (or two) messages. First the authorization, then if approved the clearing message to set the flow of funds in motion. The authorization is real-time, but the financial clearing is processed in batch files a few times per day, and per network. The frequency depends on the acquirer and per network. A majority of payments are DMS, I'll explain some use cases below.

A dual-message transaction allows a merchant to do things like:

- Cancel the authorization without needing to perform a refund in the case of an accidental charge or inability to fulfill an order.
- Adjust the amount to capture a higher amount, like with adding a tip in a restaurant. The initial use case for DMS transactions was for gas stations, where the total is not known until the customer finishes filling up their tank.
- Partially clear the transaction, as individual parts of an order ship or a service is rendered.

The separation of authorization and clearing in DMS transactions is an important separation for many merchants. A few example cases:

1) Validations. Often when a shopper adds a card on a merchant site, say for a subscription, the merchant will send a $0 or $1 "validation" authorization to check that the card is legitimate. They then either cancel or let that authorization expire. If it were an SMS transaction, they would have to refund that transaction and the shopper would see the $1 charge on their statement. While the cardholder may see the authorization hold, canceling

the authorization should release the funds more quickly than a capture request followed by a refund process.

2) Use cases where the time of purchase and the time of billing are separated – a typical example is physical goods purchased online. When a shopper clicks "buy" the authorization call is sent, and if approved sets in motion a series of systems from the OMS (order management system), warehousing, logistics partners, etc. on the merchant side. It's typical for a merchant not to clear the transaction until the parcel is ready to be shipped. This helps protect against scenarios where the item becomes out of stock, etc. If multiple parts of a single order ship at different times the merchant can also partially capture from the total authorized amount as items ship.

LIABILITY

Liability for payments can be put simply as "if this transaction ends up being fraudulent or the shopper has a valid complaint, who is *liable* for those funds?" The most common example is for chargebacks with card transactions. There are times when the merchant is liable for chargebacks and the issuer and/or network will claw back the funds. In other instances, the issuer is liable. This can happen when there's been a "liability shift," such as when the transaction went through 3D Secure, and the customer completed second factor authentication.

For card-present transactions, the issuer usually is liable for fraudulent charges. But as of 2015 that liability can shift to the merchant if the merchant fails to adopt EMV-capable terminals (chip readers).

3DS

3D Secure is a form of two-factor authentication supported by EMVCo – the consortium of card networks. It's the standard for additional security in card payments for online transactions, when a cardholder checks out, they may be prompted for 3DS after inputting their card details. The cardholder will be asked to add an additional piece of data like a one-time-password or PIN sent to them over text or email for example. From the merchant perspective, if a customer completes 3DS successfully the liability *shifts* back to the issuer, so the merchant will not be liable for fraudulent chargebacks. No liability, that sounds too good to be true!

You're right – 3DS is lovingly called the "conversion killer" by many. It adds friction for customers during checkout, both time, redirects, and the need for them to enter a password. It does not load perfectly on every device or browser. Some regions and countries have a high application of 3DS, and consumers are used to this as part of the checkout flow, others may see 3DS very rarely and drop off due to unfamiliarity. For this reason it's important for a merchant to take an optimized approach and choose when to apply 3DS. Examples include for high-value or high-risk transactions.

There are also countries where 3DS is mandated for certain transaction types. For example certain transactions in Europe due to PSD2 regulations.

3DS is only applicable on customer-initiated (CIT) transactions, where the shopper is present. For merchant-initiated (MIT) transactions like recurring or subscription charges there is no way, or expectation, for 3DS to be completed.

EMVCO

EMVCo stands for "Europay, Mastercard, Visa" – the three companies that created the standard. Now the consortium also includes JCB, American Express, Discover, and China UnionPay. It was formed in 1999 to develop and manage specifications to drive smooth, secure, and interoperable global payments. The member card brands share responsibility for the reliability and security of card transactions. They're responsible for writing common technical standards which have helped drive mass adoption of cards globally. An example of EMVCo innovation is the EMV Chip Specifications created to reduce fraud for in-person POS payments. More recently, the 3DS 2 protocol to support 3DS better in-app and digital wallets, among other payment channels.

3DS 2.0

The original 3DS protocol was created in 2001 by Visa – long before mobile checkout and in-app purchasing – so it unsurprisingly does not translate well to these devices and use cases. In 2019, 64.4 percent of global ecommerce sales happened on mobile devices. It makes sense that EMVCo felt pressure to modernize it.[5] 3DS 2.0 was designed largely to reduce the friction of 3DS that led to lower conversion rates and merchants being hesitant to prompt customers to authenticate.

3DS 2.0 provides the same fraud protections and liability shift as its predecessor, but rather than always needing cardholder engagement it has "frictionless" flows. By collecting additional data such as browser data, the issuer and 3DS risk systems are able to make more accurate authentication decisions. 3DS 2.0 analyzes more than one hundred data points.

It is purpose-built for contemporary payment environments, such as mobile. Issuing banks are able to build authentication experiences through their banking apps, for example a cardholder authenticating a payment in-app with a fingerprint or face ID. The authentication flow can be embedded in the merchant's checkout page, rather than requiring a redirect, to further decrease friction and drop-offs.

In Europe. PSD2 has helped to drive the merchant adoption of 3DS 2.0 as PSD2 mandated Strong Customer Authentication (SCA) for most online transactions. Brazil and Australia also have regulatory mandates leading to the swift adoption of 3DS 2.0. *Delegated Authentication* will be an important alternative to 3DS2 in the future; unlike 3DS, it's fully merchant controlled. It's authentication without issuer involvement, however this also means there is no liability shift. Merchants can weigh which authentication flow suits a transaction: Delegated Authentication with no liability shift and higher conversion or 3DS2 *with* a liability shift but patchy conversion.

FEES

The economics of payments are complex and opaque, some would say by design. As a heuristic, each player takes a cut – however, a majority of these fees are dictated by the card networks for credit and debit payments. Remembering that each player receives a toll for their part in a transaction means that adding additional partners, like a gateway layer rather than a direct connection to a payment method, can increase fees.

First, I'll cover the simplistic view of card transaction fees. You may hear the terms "blend" and "IC++," which are the two most common pricing models for fees. I'll break both of those down first before exploring the different categories and types of card fees those models contain.

Card fees have many components, and for many smaller merchants (like Value Added Wax) it is easier to negotiate with a provider and reconcile incoming revenue with predictable fees. Blend-structured pricing is great for merchants like this. The interchange, scheme fees, and acquiring markup fees are "blended" into one percentage fee, usually alongside a fixed fee processing or gateway fee, say $0.30.

However, like any time you use a flat fee, at scale you're likely over-paying. Still, the margins lost here may not be worth the complexity of managing more line-item fees. This also depends heavily on your card mix – different types of cards carry different interchange fees – so if you're a merchant with heavy debit volume, blend pricing may be hurting you more than a B2B merchant whose customers use corporate credit cards. In such cases, IC++ models break down all the costs of card processing into three parts: interchange fee, a scheme/card associations fee, and processing fee. Many merchants do want to see the fees broken out. Other providers will only bill this way.

So what are those specific fees that are contained in each model, whether it's blend or IC++ pricing?

AUTHORIZATION/PROCESSING FEES

These fees are assessed by their merchant's gateway, usually for each transaction or refund sent, regardless of whether it's authorized or whether the merchant captures the funds.

Interchange is the portion of payment fees collected by the Issuing bank in exchange for the value merchants get by having easy access to that Issuer's customers. Rather than have each Issuer negotiate rates, the network that that Issuer brands their cards with sets the rates. Many of the costs of creating the card payment ecosystem are realized up by Issuers: setting up programs, underwriting and assessing cardholders, managing risk, customer support, etc.

Interchange fees tend to make up the bulk of the overall cost of a payment. Annoyingly, the specific interchange fees vary widely in different geographies and transaction profiles, and the structure of these fees also change all the time. Some countries have pushed for standardization of interchange. In Europe this happened in 2015, and Australia in 2017.

For example, debit interchange in the U.S. can vary hugely depending on what kind of debit card it is. An individual debit card has an average rate of 1.5 percent, while a business debit card has an average rate of 2.4 percent. In some countries and regions interchange is capped by regulatory authorities. In the EU, for example, Interchange is capped at 0.2 percent for consumer debit cards and 0.3 percent for consumer credit cards. Australia has capped interchange at 0.88 percent.

There's a science to interchange rates. Many different aspects are taken into account when the interchange fee for a specific transaction is calculated. What effects interchange and scheme fee rates? Here's a few data points that comprise an interchange rate assessment:

- Scheme: Visa, Mastercard
- Card type: commercial credit, premium rewards cards, standard debit, etc.
- Funding source: debit, credit, prepaid store card
- Shopper interaction: POS, eCommerce, MOTO; CNP vs CP
- MCC (Merchant Category Code)
- Regionality: local, intraregional, interregional
- Additional data: like with Level 2 and Level 3 data

> **MCCS**
>
> An MCC, or Merchant Category Code, is a four-digit number assigned to any merchant processing card payments. It helps the networks understand the type of merchant and goods/services being sold in a transaction. This both helps the networks and issuing banks to assess level of risk, as well as the fees this transaction will incur.
>
> The numbers describe the primary type of business. MCC codes were created in 2004 to classify businesses, and the initial use case was to allow business card holders to more easily file 1099 tax forms. Within the context of payments, they're used by acquirers to assess risk and prohibited businesses, and the networks use them to classify interchange rates. Some very large merchants, like airlines, will even have their own MCC code.

The Networks also use interchange as a lever to incentivize behavior, for example: lowering the interchange on electronic POS transactions as a way to drive merchants to adopt electronic terminals and evolve away from paper sales drafts. Another example is increasing interchange when a merchant does not send AVS details with an online transaction, as this makes it harder for an Issuer to gauge the validity of a transaction and thus the argument can be made that the transaction is riskier. This is called a downgrade.

A **downgrade** means a higher interchange rate will apply to a transaction for not meeting specific interchange criteria. These are only relevant really for transactions issued and acquired in the U.S. The most common downgrades are late capture (after two days) and missing billing address (AVS)

LEVEL 2 AND 3 DATA

Additional data is provided by some merchants in the authorization, called Level 2 and Level 3 data. This extra data can be very helpful for certain kinds of purchases, especially B2B transactions or an airline ticket. Submitting this data can decrease interchange fees, for example in the U.S. merchants can see up to a ninety-basis point reduction in interchange on U.S. domestic transactions.

Level 2 data is tax information, like the customer code, invoice number, order number, tax amount, and tax ID number. Level 3 data is line-item data of what the charge contains, in addition to all the elements in Level 1 and Level 2 data. Merchants send receipt level data, for example the unit price, quantity, SKUs, or item codes.

Airlines are an example of when you may have interacted with Level 2 or 3 additional data. A cardholder will be able to see itinerary data in their shopper statement due to additional data passed to the issuing bank during the transaction. What about Level 1? This is the data required for any card transaction: the card number, expiration date, zip code, and billing address.

Data	Level 1	Level 2	Level 3
Merchant Name	✔	✔	✔
Transaction Amount	✔	✔	✔
Date	✔	✔	✔
Customer Code		✔	✔
Tax Amount		✔	✔
Ship From Postal Code			✔
Destination Postal Code			✔
Invoice Number			✔
Order Number			✔
Line Item Details			✔

SCHEME FEES

Scheme fees are the fees applied to transactions to compensate the networks for their role in facilitating a payment. The network has a central role connecting acquirers to issuing banks, acting as a "switch" to make sure the transactions and funds go to the correct parties. Scheme fees, like interchange, are determined by the networks.

There are multiple scheme fees applied to every transaction: they're applied at different stages of the transaction and are applied only when that event occurs. Examples: authorization fees, 3DS authentication fees, learning fees, settlement fees. They can be assessed on each transaction, but some are monthly or quarterly (FANF and TPE fees). They are not as transparent as interchange fees so many providers will show them bundled. Additionally, they are not returned on refunds the way interchange fees are.

SETTLEMENT FEES OR ACQUIRING MARKUP

This fee goes to the acquirer and is typically a percentage of the settled amount or volume of the transaction.

There can also be ancillary fees associated with payment acceptance. Below are a few basics that I consider functionally necessary.

- Risk fees: It's smart for merchants to block some transactions; a risk provider can help you decide which transactions to process. There's a huge breadth of providers offering everything from hands-off, fully managed services to tools that let merchants tune hundreds of rules to optimize risk

- Tokenization fees: If a merchant stores card details, they need to be tokenized. A few large merchants are PCI Level 1, meaning they have the infrastructure and security in place to store card details themselves. A majority of merchants don't – so they need a token vault. Many merchants will use one offered by their gateway, though some opt for a third party
- Add-on services like account updater, network tokenization, faster settlement, and other optimization tools.

TOKENIZATION

Tokenization, at the highest level, means substituting a sensitive piece of data with a non-sensitive equivalent, or token, which can be used to reference the initial piece of data.

In the world of payments, tokenization is a security measure taken for payment credentials (like card or bank account details), often allowing merchants to store token references, stay out of PCI scope, and use those tokens to process a card transaction. Merchants may tokenize cards in their own PCI compliant vault, use a 3rd party, or tokenize with their payment partner. In the event of a data breach, the token is useless to a fraudster as it cannot be used to authorize or initiate a transaction.

Using a provider for card detail tokenization can greatly reduce operational and actual costs for a merchant, some estimate the total cost of PCI-DSS compliance in the US is several billion dollars. Reputational risk alongside a data breach is also a reason for merchants to outsource tokenization if they don't have the capability to adequately secure card credentials.

Most gateways will offer tokenization either included in their other services or as a standalone add-on service. However, some merchants have multiple payment partners. For these merchants, they would either need to tokenize the same card across multiple providers and manage that logic internally or bifurcate customers to one or the other provider. This adds complexity, duplication, ongoing maintenance, and makes it difficult to recognize the same shopper across their different providers. For these merchants a true 3rd party token vault may make the most sense. This is a provider that acts as their token vault, allowing the merchant to stay outside of PCI scope, but the tokens do not tie them to an individual provider. The downside is added cost, another partnership and integration to manage, another point of failure, and potentially added latency to individual transactions.

CROSS-BORDER PAYMENTS

Thanks to global supply chains and shipping, commerce is global, and merchants don't always have a formal presence (read: entity) in every country where they have shoppers or accept payments. Cross border payments are any payments where a party in one country wants to pay a party in another – say a merchant in Canada wants to allow a shopper in Spain to buy their goods. Many merchants want to expand their businesses across the globe and attract more customers. Cross-border payments allow for this, merchants can reach shoppers anywhere and generate additional revenue, from almost any country, in their local currency. Experts project cross-border shopping will make up 20 percent of all ecommerce in 2022, leading to sales of $630 billion.[6]

The SEPA (Single Euro Payments Area) payments system in Europe is an effort to resolve the issue of cross-border payments in a region that shares a currency. If you wanted to send a payment from Italy to Germany payments systems in both Italy and Germany would have to be involved in the transaction. SEPA created debit and credit systems that banks in SEPA countries could belong to directly.

CROSS-BORDER ACQUIRING

Cross-border acquiring means any card transaction that happens where the merchant is in a different country than the customer, and so the payment crosses international lines. While a cross-border transaction may appear quite smooth to a customer, or even to a merchant, behind the scenes they're a complex web. Multiple players, two (or more) currencies, compliance with local government and international regulations, and risks. Additional fees may apply, like taxes and duties, as well as fees from issuing banks for the currency foreign exchange.

Fees are a key consideration when acquiring card transactions cross-border. Card fees are regulated in many countries, so in some instances fees could be higher cross-border, yet lower in other scenarios.

If a merchant outside of Japan wants to sell to customers in Japan and present the transaction (and process it) in JPY, the fees can be less than if they processed that transaction with a local Japanese entity. The inverse is true in Europe – if a merchant uses a US entity to offer EUR pricing to a cardholder in the EU, the payment fees will be higher than if that merchant used a local EU entity due to the interchange caps in Europe.

Where you cross-border from, if you're a merchant with multiple entities, can have many impacts. For example, a merchant with EU and US entities may decide to use their EU entity to process in Canada to benefit from interchange caps.

Network/scheme rules dictate that to acquire card transactions locally a merchant must have a local presence (entity). To get around this, there are some providers who act as the "merchant of record" locally, on behalf of the foreign merchant.

However, not all payment methods require a local entity – many non-card methods do not. This means a merchant does not need a local entity nor do they need to manage that local currency. The payment method or payment provider (PSP) (if they don't directly connect to the payment method) can often settle the merchant in their preferred local currency. Note, then the partner performs the FX. More on the considerations of this below.

This is particularly interesting because, as noted above, cards account for 47 percent of the ecommerce payments in the US – and the more merchants who adopt non-card local methods not only benefit by increasing the potential customers but also can do so with more speed than opening local entities.

CORRESPONDENT BANKING

How do funds actually move across borders? When two banks enter an agreement together to become international correspondents, they open what's known as *nostro* and *vostro* accounts in each other's banks. I'll explain these more below. They then can transfer money from that account into another domestic account in the same country. In such correspondent banking scenarios, the banks agree to all sorts of terms like minimum balances, overdraft allowances, transaction fees, etc. These reciprocal accounts can be used to transfer funds in what appears as "cross border" but is not, mechanically, the case.

They usually use SWIFT to communicate these transactions. As you can imagine, this isn't a perfect balance of ins/outs. When a bank has more funds than they need in their correspondent account, they can loan it, use it, or trade the currency for one they have more demand for.

Correspondent banking doesn't always have to be two-party either. Some larger money transmitters can manage the bank accounts and balances across multiple banks in multiple countries themselves, and perform wire transfers, for example, to balance the accounts. An example of this is the card networks (Visa, MasterCard, American Express), who maintain balances in every country they operate in to be able to support the flow of funds in and out of the accounts of their bank customers (Issuers).

Let's say a customer of Bank A in one country needs to pay for products they purchased from a supplier in a different country. Bank A determines the foreign exchange rate to calculate the amount in the seller's currency and deducts that amount from the customer's account. Bank A instructs Bank B (seller's bank) – the correspondent bank – to pay out that amount to the supplier from Bank A's account with Bank B. Bank A's account is the correspondent account with a foreign bank (Bank B). This is also referred to as the "nostro" account, the money a bank has on deposit at another bank.

Bank A likely doesn't just have a correspondent relationship with Bank B, however. Many banks establish multiple correspondent relationships across the globe to allow international transactions where they don't have a physical presence. Large banks might have hundreds of correspondent relationships.

SWIFT

SWIFT stands for the Society for Worldwide Interbank Financial Telecommunications — it's the message format that over eleven *thousand* financial institutions globally use to coordinate the cross-border movement of money between more than two hundred countries. Trillions of dollars a day are moved with the norms set by SWIFT.

It's important to note that SWIFT is not in the flow of funds; it does not act as the clearing or settlement mechanism. It enables associated banks to communicate, send, and record messages. Correspondent banking is what moves funds between accounts, alongside the SWIFT messages.

SWIFT has been in the news recently because Russia was kicked out of the network in February 2022 due to its invasion of Ukraine. The outcome of blocking Russia from SWIFT means huge volumes of international transactions — importers and exporters — need to find another way to transact. Europe in particular relies heavily on Russian energy exports, so without an easy way to transfer funds, aspects of the global economy could grind to a halt. Cross border money movement won't stop; it just may be slow and difficult.

PROS, CONS, CONSIDERATIONS

There are many aspects to consider from the merchant perspective when deciding whether to localize payments. The following is not a conclusive list but should give you enough to understand the types of considerations and trade-offs.

Currency Implications

Firstly, and most obvious, is the FX or Foreign Exchange consideration. If a merchant is from the US and processing payments in Canada, they will be receiving funds in CAD. If a merchant has no need for holding large sums of CAD, for example they do not have enough local spend in the form of employees, vendors, and office space, they will want to exchange that to a more relevant currency, in this case USD. Their bank will charge them both a fee for this service as well as baking in additional cost to the exchange rate used.

Cash Management

Second but related is the need for cash management. This goes beyond the above costs associated with FX and into operational costs. This may mean needing to set up additional bank accounts, hire teams to manage these relationships and balances, and the surrounding regulations.

Some countries have currency controls where there is a high tax to take funds out of a country. If a merchant wants to present and charge customers in a local currency, they may run into additional taxes and fees to repatriate the revenue. Brazil and Argentina are both examples of this. Some merchants consider this a cost of doing business and serving these customers locally, others consider creative solutions. My favorite example of this is a "solution" I've heard explored by two separate merchants. Argentina has a high tax to take currency out of the country, higher than the tax to export many other goods. Rumor has it there are companies who found that purchasing cattle and wine in Argentina, exporting them to a nearby country with lesser currency controls, and selling the goods cost less overall than simply exchanging funds out of the country.

Localization Rules

Another important thing to consider is various localization rules. For local acquiring of card transactions a merchant must have a local entity. But there are other possible regulations, for example in certain countries to sell physical goods or services, like car share or gig economy platforms, a merchant *must* have a local presence.

Some countries also require payments data to be localized – like India and Russia – though compliance falls more to payments processors than individual merchants.

Authorization Rates

The rule of thumb is that authorization rates on local acquiring connections are higher. An obvious reason is that the issuing banks are better able to assess the risk of transactions for local merchants using local acquiring banks, not to mention that an overseas transaction could easily be with a stolen card.

Some countries, like India, have huge authorization rate benefits to localization. There's a so-called 30/60/90 rule – with cross-border acquiring a merchant may only see a 30 percent authorization rate. That could double, going up to 60 percent if they included 3DS in their authorization. To get to 90 percent authorization rates, a merchant should have a *local* entity, do local acquiring, and use 3DS. Japan is the opposite side of the spectrum where cross-border authorization rates can be close or equal to those of locally acquired transaction authorization rates. An increase in authorization rates means more revenue, which may offset the increased fees from FX and operational complexity.

Fees

Fees may also be lower for localized transactions, such as the scheme and interchange fees. If a merchant isn't able to localize in every country where they want to accept payments, there is a way to still optimize fees. Some countries have capped payment fees, like interchange in Europe or Australia. So for example a merchant in the US who also has an EU entity may decide to process cross-border transactions in Canada through the EU instead. There are many deep nuances here but I'm using this example to illustrate why it makes sense for merchants to explore these options when launching in a new geography. Some payment providers can also provide guidance on modeling out cost implications.

Section Two –
Non-Card Taxonomy

In the U.S., cash and cards are king. However, go beyond the U.S. and the payment landscape looks drastically different. There are many reasons for this, a large one is the points culture of American cards does not exist to the same extent in other countries, meaning there is less of a benefit for cardholders to use cards to pay. Some regions and countries with large unbanked populations have hopscotched straight to mobile wallets. In Germany, where cash is predominant and getting a credit card is often an undertaking, debit and online banking are more common for online purchases.

There's huge variation globally in the way people pay, from cash, to cards, to vouchers, to QR codes, to wallets, to virtual accounts, and everything in between. Maybe you're a giant nerd like me and reading this out of pure interest. Or maybe you're a merchant trying to localize in foreign countries. Understanding how your customers prefer to pay is necessary to a true localization effort. Or maybe you're the next great entrepreneur dreaming up a better payment method. This section should give you some new perspectives and perhaps a model or two as a jumping off point.

In an increasingly globalized world it makes sense to understand how people pay beyond cards. If you're a merchant wanting to expand to new geographies, you should offer payment methods that are familiar to your customers.

Card penetration can vary widely. In Japan, 65% of online transactions are with cards, while in China 21% of online payments are with card, in large part due to the ubiquity of wallet payments. In the Netherlands, for example, bank transfers via iDeal are the most common way to pay. Some debit cards don't even have a PAN printed on the back because they were created just to be used in-store.

In Asia, a vast ecosystem of digital wallets has become the predominant way to pay. In Brazil, and many other countries, paying for an online transaction with cash is supported and normal, as is paying in installments over cards. In a globalized world, you may have customers everywhere. Allow them to pay how they'd like.

But from my experience working with merchants, non-card forms of payment can be daunting. The flows are different, and functionality is varied – for example, not every method offers refunds, the ability for the consumer to dispute a transaction (like a chargeback for a card payment), and settlement delays can be a nightmare for accounts receivable teams if not understood in advance.

I think breaking down non-card payment methods into a few themes helps make them much more approachable. I call this the **taxonomy of payment methods**. Whether you're talking about Virtual Accounts in Indonesia or Oxxo in Mexico, you'll see that both methods have quite a few similarities. Here's the taxonomy I like to use:

- Bank based methods
  - ▷ Direct Debit
  - ▷ Online Banking

    ▷ RTP
    ▷ Checks
- Delayed Payments
- Wallets
- Cash/ATM
- Crypto

BANK-BASED PAYMENT METHODS

There are a lot of ways to pay with a bank account, whether it's direct debit or online banking, B2B ACH or Wires, or checks. Some are days-long processes that are just a step above manual; others are modern, real-time systems. I'm going to describe the key types and concepts in this section and dive into a few examples.

A key governing concept of bank payments is *push versus pull*. Does the payee pull the funds, or does the payer push them? Put more simply: does the customer send funds (push), or do they give the merchant/seller their banking info to let them pull those funds? This distinction is important and says a lot about a bank-based payment method.

Push methods do not bounce because the sending bank already knows whether the customer has funds because they have to login and authenticate their banking details. **Pull payments** on the other hand, like ACH or other direct debits, can bounce because the customer puts in their details and then the merchant reaches out for those funds. Rather than the customer logging in and sending the funds (initiating or pushing the authorization to the merchant), the customer is giving the merchant their details to go and pull those funds.

It's like a paper check, in essence – here you can run into things like insufficient funds. Checks, cards, and ACH Direct Debit are all Pull methods. Wire transfers, online banking, and RTP are push.

DIRECT DEBIT

A direct debit is "permission to pull" – an individual or entity provides a merchant with their banking details and permission to withdraw funds directly from their account under specified terms (monthly subscription, rent payments, etc.). Once a merchant or entity is authorized, they can automatically take payments from your account.

Direct debit can be used for regular bills of varying amounts, like utilities, or fixed subscriptions of the same amount, like gym memberships. Direct debit, unsurprisingly, was used for 1.2 percent of global ecommerce payments in 2020.[7]

In 1964, Direct Debit was created by Unilever as a way to collect money from ice cream shops, rather than the existing options of cash, check, or standing order at a bank. Direct Debit enabled the payer to give permission to the payee to take regular payments directly from their bank account. In the intervening fifty years, it grew in popularity enough to account for 20 percent of all cashless payments in the EU by 2016, according to payment statistics from the European Central Bank. It's a convenient method for bill pay, especially given its automatic nature, compared to mailing a check or paying with a card.

ACH, which stands for "automated clearing house," is the direct debit rail in the U.S. It grew out of check processing in the 1970s, though while checks are pull – ACH supports both push and pull. In 2020 alone more than $62 trillion was processed over ACH. ACH is a bank-owned utility, Nacha (National Automated Clearing House Association) is responsible for managing regulation and rules. Nacha is a non-profit network of banks that joined together to enable easy movement of funds between the banks using account and routing numbers, and a batch process. It also is the body that enforces rules for over 10,000 of the member banks and participants. These rules apply to all ACH participants like payment processors, businesses, and individuals who use the method.

GUARANTEED ACH

A more recent innovation to make up for some of the shortcomings of ACH transactions is so-called "guaranteed" ACH. There are a few flavors of this – but, in short, the effort is to reduce the insufficient funds (NSF) risk related to ACH. Reversibility is a large concern for pull-based payment methods, as confirmations are asynchronous, and the account holder may no longer have necessary funds by the time the transaction is processed by their bank. There are two key use cases where this is a powerful solution, the first is when funding accounts, like adding funds to a brokerage account or a neobank offering direct debit early access for paychecks. A trading platform can give a user instant access to their funds to trade on the platform even though their bank account will not clear the transaction for a few days. The second is to reduce credit limit increase fraud. This is when someone pays down a credit card bill, they're given access to their refreshed credit line before the ACH fully clears, they rack up more charges, and then the initial transaction to pay off the balance is reversed.

Individual companies may build out guaranteed ACH in house, which amounts to a risk system to understand a user, their history of NSF declines, ping their account for a balance inquiry, and make an informed decision based on those data points. There are also companies now building Guaranteed ACH as a standalone product for other companies to embed, often as a credit risk score.

In Europe, SEPA (Single Euro Payments Area) is the Direct Debit rail. It works alongside the online banking services in individual European countries, like Sofort in Germany and iDeal in the Netherlands. Many European countries prefer bank transfer methods to debit or credit cards, so SEPA is a great way for merchants with recurring models – like streaming subscriptions – to support recurring payments. The first transaction will be with a customer's online bank, as a "push" transaction, but the merchant stores the banking details for subsequent direct debit "pull" transactions over SEPA.

RISK AND REVERSIBILITY

Direct debit transactions don't have an authentication layer, like 3DS or a CVV check. For this reason fraud is a key consideration. Additionally, reversals can be hard to defend against. With SEPA, for example, a shopper can perform a chargeback and reverse the charge for eight weeks after the transaction date and the merchant has no recourse to dispute the chargeback beyond directly contacting the customer. Additionally, a SEPA transaction can be charged back even if a refund has been processed – unlike a card transaction. NACHA

Unlike card methods, direct debit is also not authorized in real time. It can take a few days for a merchant to receive a response that the transaction is complete, and then often a few additional days for settlement of those funds. This is especially relevant for merchants selling physical goods who should wait for a confirmation of the transaction before shipping items.

Direct debit is the backbone of B2B payments, and any larger, recurring transactions such as payroll, bill pay, vendor payments. More than 82 percent of electronic payments in the U.S. are processed over ACH. It's extremely cost effective when compared to payment methods like credit cards which are prohibitively expensive for large transaction sizes, Direct Debit often costs just a few cents to send.

While a great option compared to cash or check, in relation to other digital forms of payment direct debit has a few weaknesses. Payments take a few days to clear (or settle). BACS in the UK is typically five days, SEPA in the EU is three. Additionally, it can take a few days before a merchant knows that a payment has failed – the common reason being insufficient funds. Fraud is also an issue with direct debit

We'll cover this in more depth in the B2B chapter later. ACH is also extremely cost effective compared to say card transactions, especially for high ticket transactions: often a transaction will cost a fraction of a penny.

ONLINE BANKING

Online banking is seemingly straightforward: a way for a shopper to pay online, with the funds in their bank account. A shopper initiates the payment from their bank account to a third-party like a merchant – they "push" the funds. This push can be to another bank account they own, a friend's bank account, or a company's account. Thankfully, for our understanding, online banking as a payment method tends to work the same in most countries.

These "push" methods are sometimes also referred to as a "bank redirect" method – because a shopper is redirected to their bank portal so they can complete the payment and push funds to the merchant. This can sometimes require multiple web page redirects, or for mobile commerce, an app switch to the relevant banking app, and ideally a switch back to the browser or merchant app when the transaction is complete.

Most countries have their own online banking methods, often a consortium of the banks in that country. For example, iDEAL in the Netherlands, ACH bank transfer in the U.S., and Interac in Canada.

Like direct debit, online banking payments can be slow. Additionally, due to the involvement of redirects, there tends to be negative impacts on conversion. It's more likely that a shopper will drop off at each redirect. These additional steps also increase the likelihood of a page not loading or a customer not being redirected back correctly or in a timely manner. Redirect online banking payment methods create more friction for the shopper to complete the transaction, thus increasing the chances of incomplete transactions.

Furthermore, in some countries, like the Philippines, the online banking rails are only open during normal banking hours, 9am to 5pm. In Malaysia online banking is offline between midnight and 1am for their reconciliation processes. Sometimes a bank may be offline in a country, for whatever reason, and a shopper may wonder why they cannot complete a transaction. The shopper must be present to authenticate the transaction, so there's no option for the merchant to queue the transaction, like with storing and retrying a card transaction.

DEEP DIVE: OPEN BANKING IN THE UNITED KINGDOM

In Europe, with PSD2, banks were required to create APIs for third parties to initiate payments for their customers. In the U.K. specifically, there was a regulatory mandate for U.K. banks to offer open APIs.

The point of open banking is to simplify and standardize how financial information is accessed and shared, allowing for increased competition and more innovation in financial services. From a payments perspective, open banking allows for smoother online banking transactions between customers and merchants. Shoppers select their bank on the merchant's site and are redirected to authenticate the transaction. Third parties, like a payment provider, can build integrations to the banks and offer merchants a more seamless online banking integration.

REAL-TIME PAYMENTS

Real-time payments are a growing global trend. They're meant to overcome some of the time inconsistency and settlement delay issues that frequent typical online bank payments. I consider this method a subset of online banking, but it's distinct enough to warrant its own section.

Many countries are developing these systems at a national level. They are real-time; always online twenty-four hours a day, seven days a week, and 365 days a year; and have messaging as well to confirm completion of a transaction – unlike ACH and checks

Faster payments, or RTRP (real-time retail payments) are push methods. Examples of RTRP are UPI in India, RTP in the U.S., Faster Payments in the U.K., TIPS in Tanzania, Pix in Brazil, and Blik in Poland, among others.

Here I'll go into UPI and Pix in depth, framing them as illustrative examples. In a later chapter, I'll cover real-time payments in the U.S. in more depth.

UPI

India's real-time payment system, called UPI or United Payments Interface, was created by the National Payments Corporation of India. Like in the U.K., UPI is an example of open banking. However, there are very key differences in both approach and adoption.

UPI stems from the Indian government's "Digital India" initiative. It has the goal of digitizing and pushing for cashless payments across the country, in part to improve the ability to track the flow of money in the economy and reduce tax evasion. In less than five years, it's become the predominant payment method. In 2021, it accounted for 10 percent of all retail payments. In October 2021 alone, UPI processed 4.2 billion transactions, equating to over $100 billion in processed volume.

UPI benefits from being imagined and engineered in the internet age for transactions as they exist today: many are peer-to-peer (P2P) and online.

There are a few components of the initiative, like the creation of the NPCI – National Payments Corporation of

India. The NPCI developed UPI as a payment method, with BHIM (Bharat Interface for Money) as the payment app to modernize digital transactions. Regulators require all merchants that transact more than five hundred million INR (Indian rupee) per year accept UPI and RuPay payments, which pushed huge merchant adoption.

The push for demonetization in India in 2016 also set the stage for digital payments when the government deprecated the INR 500 and INR 100 notes. This move was in large part to curb the underground economy, giving the government more visibility into transactions and thus collecting taxes. To stand in for the decrease in the cash economy there needed to be a method that had similar utility – instant, cheap to use, and ubiquitous. UPI accomplishes that in many ways by being low cost, offering instant confirmation and settlement, and carrying a very low risk of transactions being reversed.

We know what UPI is, but how does it work?

Each user registers a VPA or "Virtual Payment Address" with their bank. You can think of this as an alternative to the routing and bank account numbers used in the U.S. Rather than being a long string, the VPA can be short and memorable.

During a transaction the VPA is used to lookup the account holder, a real-time authorization occurs, and the account holder performs authentication over SMS or push notification.

Another important aspect of the VPA, beyond being more memorable and user-friendly for payments, is that it's useless on its own. While a bank account and routing number in the wrong hands can be used fraudulently, the VPA cannot.

PIX

Pix is one of the newer RTP systems globally – it was launched in November of 2020 by the Central Bank of Brazil. This new payments system is operated by the issuers and wallets in Brazil, and 62 percent of the Brazilian population was registered as of November 2021, truly meteoric growth in a single year. By mid-2021 more than 55.4 percent of Brazilians had used Pix for an online purchase.

Pix was built to democratize access to digital payments, whether P2P, consumer payments, or B2B. More than 88 percent of Brazilians with cell phones have access to the internet, and eight in ten Brazilians older than ten have a cell phone.[8] However, nearly 30 percent of Brazilians are unbanked – Pix allows users to link digital wallets, not just bank accounts.

Like UPI, Pix does away with the need to share bank accounts and routing numbers. For P2P payments a user can provide their phone number, their CPF (tax ID number), email address, or a Pix code that is randomly generated.

To pay with Pix, a user can either complete a transaction with QR code or copy and paste a code. That user can link whichever bank accounts or wallets they want to use for Pix transactions – they're able to add up to five. When initiating a transaction, the user is able to specify which linked account to pay with, allowing great interoperability across an individual's balance and different bank accounts.

Pix offers instant settlement (well, in up to ten seconds) and is online twenty-four hours a day, seven days a week, 365 days a year. Compared to the thirty-day settlement delay for card payments in Brazil, Pix is extremely merchant and user friendly. It's also much cheaper than bank transfers and card fees, which explains the rapid adoption of the system by merchants as well.

CHECKS

So where do checks fit in? How many countries are they still relevant in even? I mean, it is 2022, after all. In the U.S. checks are still very relevant. In fact, it's one of the few countries that still relies heavily on them. In 2018, sixteen billion checks were written in the U.S., amounting to $26.2 trillion. I use checks monthly; yeah, that's right – I said *monthly*. The simplest way for me to transfer funds between two of my accounts at different banks is to cut myself a check and use mobile deposit.

I'm not going to go into too much depth on checks. Yes, they exist. Yes, they are still widely prevalent. Yes, I still pay a shocking number of my bills via check. This is also a very U.S.-based quirk. To the neobanks: yes, you'll probably need to support checks or check processing. To everyone else: if you've never used a check, it's unlikely you'll really need to in the future.

Although checks feel quite outdated today with all of our digital forms of payment, they really were the first interoperable way to pay. You could have a payer with a different bank than the payee's bank, and a check would allow funds to flow between those two different banks. Another interesting feature of checks is that they clear "at par," meaning there's no interchange taken. The funds the account holder pays to the merchant or individual are the funds that they receive. There's no loss to fees. This makes checks functionally a free form of payment.

Checks are "permission to pull" transactions, giving the routing and account number and your permission for the recipient to pull funds. Insufficient funds are unsurprisingly a key issue – by the time someone goes to pull the funds from the payer's account, sometimes there are insufficient funds in the account.

In 2004, the Check Clearing for the 21st Century Act – referred to as Check 21 – was passed. It gave banks the ability to create digital images of checks, which could then be sent electronically for processing. A main goal was to reduce the costs associated with paper check processing, especially the need to physically transport the checks. At one point in time, the Federal Reserve had a fleet of jets, at times over 100, to transport checks across the country daily. Billions of dollars of checks would be shuttled to tarmacs and loaded onto jets at day's end to be redistributed to the relevant banks in other cities and states. In 1995, the Federal Reserve spent over $35 million on the logistics of moving checks alone.

This cost wasn't the impetus for modernizing check processing, though. It took the disruption to air travel directly following the 9/11 attacks to force a change. For a week after 9/11, all air travel was shut down domestically, which led to a crisis as checks backed up. Check 21 came out of that minor crisis to allow fully electronic clearing of checks.

The outcome of Check 21 is broader than operational efficiency, though. Another benefit was shortening float. One working paper by the Fed estimates that the impact to the banking system is $1.2 billion a year, with an additional $2 billion in benefits for consumers and businesses.[9]

DELAYED PAYMENTS

I'm combining BNPL (buy now, pay later), open invoice, and installments into one "type" – "delayed payments," whether that's a standard cadence of repayments, or fourteen days later in one lump sum. Under this "type" the shopper receives their goods before they've paid in full.

Within this taxonomy there are two subtypes: one where the merchant is paid as shoppers complete payments, and one where the merchant receives funds up front. There are other distinctions as well to consider. Does the shopper pay interest on the loan? Is it a credit event? This is a particularly important distinction in the U.S.

Some history first. Installment plans have essentially been around as long as large purchases have been a reality, think the "layaway" model where a down payment is made then the rest is paid off over time. Think about the convenience of such a model for paying for furniture, farm equipment, or cars. While the majority of the use cases for early installments have evolved into credit cards, installments have stayed common for some industries. B2B payments, for example, rely heavily on the model still.

Installments as we know them today really got their start in 1840 for pianos, elegant furniture, and sewing machines. Singer Sewing Machines are credited with driving the consumer understanding and interest in installments – their innovative credit plan had the tagline in the 1890s: "dollar down, dollar a week."[10]

MERCHANT PAID OVER TIME

Installment payments have a strong history in Latin America. They began as agreements between consumers and individual retailers to make larger purchases possible for low-income consumers and those without formal credit or bank accounts. Whether at the point of sale or online, offering installment options is essentially mandatory for global companies doing business in Latin America and will help improve conversion rates and foster greater loyalty among these consumers.

This type of installment is popular in Brazil and Mexico. In Brazil, for example, the installment is processed by the card networks, and the merchant is settled by the networks as the shopper's payment is cleared. One workaround that some merchants may use is called "advancements" or "acceleration" of funds. This is common due to the thirty-day settlement delay in Brazil, in addition to the prevalence of installments.

To accelerate settled funds, the acquiring bank settles the merchant before the funds have cleared in the system, charging an interest rate on top for the service. For some merchant use cases, this is a huge value add despite the cost – in part because cash flow may be tight. For other merchants, waiting for the funds to clear from the shopper and networks makes more sense than paying an additional fee for faster funds.

Installments can also be supported by the issuers in some regions. Another fascinating aspect of the Brazilian payments landscape is the prevalence of installments. While BNPL was having a moment in the U.S. in 2020, in Brazil a merchant doesn't need to add a separate payment method to offer installments to a shopper. They can specify the number of installments in the authorization request, and the issuing bank manages the installment billing.

In Brazil, a merchant can specify in the authorization request how many installments the transaction should be broken into, and the issuer handles billing on the specified cadence. The downside here, however, is that the merchant only receives funds when each installment is settled in due course which causes cash flow and accounting complexity. A merchant could theoretically wait a year to be paid in full if they've offered twelve monthly installments. So while the merchant does not need to integrate another payment method, contract, or share revenue with the third party, they do have more financial risk exposure, and potentially more contact with customers to recoup failed installment payments.

Open invoice is a way of paying that's popular in some European countries. Here a shopper checks out but isn't charged until fourteen to twenty-eight days after their goods are delivered. It's a very buyer-friendly way to pay. Shoppers get to try what they've purchased and decide if they want to keep it or make returns, then are only charged for what they decide to keep.

Open invoice grew out of the catalog era of shopping. Large mail order companies would let shoppers try something before payment. If a shopper didn't like a purchase, they could return it within those fourteen days generally. Klarna, the Swedish fintech giant, began as an open invoice payment method. They helped encourage online shopping by supporting this low-risk, "try before you buy" behavior for ecommerce. Open invoice is also very popular in Germany – 63 percent of online purchases are made using the method and 90 percent of merchants in Germany offer open invoicing.[11]

From the merchant perspective, open invoice can be tricky. Unsurprisingly, the rate of returns for open invoice purchases is extremely high, upwards of 50 percent in some markets. A higher rate of returns also means a higher cost operationally and logistically to service those returns. In addition, the merchant is not paid until after the customer decides to keep the goods, meaning the merchant is out revenue for a few weeks. On top of all that, there's also a large risk of fraud. Payment providers like RatePAY offer merchants a full-payment guarantee to lessen the risk of open invoice non-payment.

Klarna, whose name is now synonymous with BNPL, began under the name Kreditor in 2005. The founders' first product was B2B factoring – they would buy receivables to give companies a cash advance and take a large cut to offset the risk they took. They pivoted into being a consumer-focused company as an open invoice payment method, allowing shoppers to receive goods from an online transaction first, and pay fourteen days later directly to Klarna – typically with a bank transfer. Rather than waiting for the shopper to complete the transaction, they would be settled more quickly.

In Sweden, and many Nordic countries, credit cards have low adoption and consumer debt carries cultural stigma. The convenience of being able to try a product before paying for it really resonated with the market, especially for retail purchases. It's explicitly not a credit product, and how it was marketed is considered a factor in their success. Klarna paid merchants at the time of order, both then taking on the risk of shopper non-payment while closing the cash-flow issue for merchants.

Overall, Klarna is a great example to transition us to the next flavor of delayed payments: where a merchant is paid up front.

MERCHANT PAID UP FRONT

Buy now, pay later (BNPL) is gaining popularity in multiple countries as a flexible way for consumers to pay overtime. BNPL transactions are often interest-free installment plans that a shopper adopts at point-of-checkout (sometimes referred to as point-of-sale, but I personally find that confusing with in-store "point of sale" terminology) to pay off a purchase or invoice over mutually agreed terms such as time, cadence, and amount of each repayment. Most BNPL providers have a minimum or maximum amount a shopper is able to use the method for and some are interest-free for consumers. The merchant receives full funds up front from the BNPL provider, who takes on custody of the debt with the shopper.

Collections rates and bad debt vary heavily from market to market. Sweden, for example, where Klarna originated, has a very strong credit mechanism. It's very straightforward to find a person's number, and all their debts are allocated to it. Also, given the cultural stigma of debt, the repayment rates in Nordic countries for BNPL are very high – in the mid to high 90 percentile. Other countries have much lower rates of collection and less unified consumer data. Some see rates in the 60-65 percent range, which inherently changes the business model for BNPL.

From a merchant cash flow perspective, BNPL is similar to cards. However, getting approved for a BNPL purchase can be easier for many shoppers than applying and getting accepted for a credit card. Some may require a soft credit check for new consumers signing up, while others underwrite new users in other ways. It also provides a delayed payment option for shoppers who cannot or do not want to have a credit card.

According to research by Kaleido Intelligence, by 2025 ecommerce spend in Europe via BNPL is predicted to hit $347 billion, constituting 30 percent of all predicted ecommerce spend in that year.[12] Global BNPL volume was $93 billion in 2020 and could hit $181 billion by 2022, according to Bloomberg. Furthermore, 39 percent of Americans say they've tried BNPL at least once, according to an early 2021 survey conducted by the Strawhecker Group.[13]

Funds immediately, says the merchant, what's the catch? Typically, a higher fee than a credit card transaction for the merchant. BNPL providers charge merchants an MDR (merchant discount rate, a blended fee) ranging from 2-6 percent. Despite this high rate – especially when you consider that BNPL transactions are for more expensive items, and thus a higher percentage MDR adds up quickly – merchants have been fast to offer BNPL. Why? Studies and sales teams have shown that consumers spend 55 percent more when using BNPL, so the higher cost to the merchants is offset by higher overall sales, outweighing the price increase for that transaction.[14] Additionally, it increases the pool of potential customers for a merchant by offering delayed payments. Overall these incremental uplifts can drive increased revenue.

From a shopper's perspective, BNPL is very similar to the installment model described in Brazil. They complete a payment monthly (or another cadence) and receive goods up front. Additionally, BNPL is a great way to serve shoppers who don't have credit cards. In Europe, just 33.7 percent of people older than fifteen have a credit card, and nearly half of all Americans in their twenties don't have a credit card.[15] The average spend on a U.K. Klarna transaction is 75 pounds ($104), which also differentiates it from the standard use case of installment purchases – to offset the impact of a large purchase.[16] Users create an account with the BNPL provider, usually link their card or bank account, and are debited the agreed amount automatically. As a user makes on-time repayments, their spending limit with that BNPL provider usually grows. In Q1 2021, Afterpay reported that 91 percent of sales were from repeat customers. Another plus of BNPL compared to traditional credit cards is that most BNPL providers only perform a *soft* credit check on a user when they sign up. This means that there is not an effect on that user's credit score when signing up.

The BNPL space is managed by third parties that take custody of the transaction from merchants, manage the billing, delinquencies, and contact with the customers. This is merchant friendly as they're able to receive funds for goods sold in a matter of days while also benefiting from increased sales – shoppers tend to spend more when given the option to pay over time. Peloton, the stationary tech-enabled bike company, and Affirm, a BNPL provider, partnered to allow Peloton riders to pay over time for equipment. Given how expensive their products are, their tech-enabled stationary bike is over $1,400, BNPL makes their product more approachable. In 2021 over 20% of Affirm's revenue came from the Peloton partnership alone.

BNPL is not without controversies, though – some of the spicier takes include it being payday lending with colorful branding, a wolf in millennial pink clothing. The fears of BNPL causing increased unmanageable debt don't feel that different than the spend one can rack up on a credit card, or across multiple credit cards. But debt is debt, and BNPL does give shoppers an easier way to spend beyond their means. Think of BNPL as "credit a la carte." Terms vary among BNPL providers, so customer understanding and clarity of terms are extremely important. Additionally, most BNPL methods don't help build a user's credit in the way a credit card repayment does – though this could change in the future.

WALLETS

Mention the term "wallets" to payments people and you quickly realize there are 1,001 definitions. I'm going to try to parse some of the most common ones out for you. This section won't go into so-called "merchant" wallets – think Amazon Pay or Shop Pay – which are a "wallet" of a customer's stored cards that the merchant has tokenized for use on their platform, or, with the example of Amazon Pay, they can then pass those details to a third-party merchant.

We've seen an explosion of wallet popularity and variety over the past few years – but it all started with Coca-Cola. They're credited with processing the first mobile wallet payment in 1997. Coca-Cola created a special vending machine in Finland where a customer could pay for their drink over text message. Fast forward to today, and digital wallets accounted for 44.5 percent of all online transaction volume in 2020, according to a Worldpay Global Payments Report. China is the country with the biggest adoption of wallets: a spectacular 72.1 percent of all online transactions in 2020 were with digital wallets.

TAXONOMY

First, there's the "wallet" a merchant may refer to – the to-kenized cards they attribute to a single account or shopper. When a customer logs into their account with a merchant, they see a list of stored cards. This can be considered a wallet. This isn't the use case I'll be exploring in this chapter, though, as stated above. In this chapter, I'll be introducing you to the types of wallets that are forms of payment themselves. There's a key question with wallets: does the wallet hold a user's funds?

The first question is if the operator of the wallet holds funds. If the answer is yes, it's a *staged* wallet. The wallet holder adds funds via a bank account, cash, or card. If the answer is no, and the wallet holds payment credentials like a card number or bank account details, it's a *pass-through* wallet. Some wallets offer both options, but knowing the difference is an important distinction.

In the U.S., we're very used to card-backed wallets like Apple and Google Pay. These tokenize (using a network to-ken, more on that later) your credit card so it can be used for in-person POS or frictionless mobile checkout. Other wallets store funds – like Venmo. A user can top up their account with a bank transfer, a card payment, or cash in some examples – once onboarded to the wallet, the user can spend these funds wherever the wallet is accepted. Closed- and open-loop also apply here! An open-loop wallet would be Venmo or Apple Cash. A closed-loop staged digital wallet example is the Starbucks balance for in-app pre-ordering of coffee.

PASS-THROUGH WALLETS

Pass-through wallets are fairly straightforward: the wallet acts as the consumer-facing provider who stores their payment details. This wallet then acts as a third party that shares those details with a merchant so the transaction can be processed. Flow-wise, sometimes the detail is shared, then the merchant processes the transaction. Other times, the merchant sends details to the wallet for them to perform the transaction. In this case, the wallet would settle funds to the merchant directly. Different flows are worth understanding in depth if you plan to offer a wallet as a merchant.

An area worth digging into in more depth is called *network tokenization.* This is how Apple Pay and Google Pay were able to revolutionize frictionless card payments on mobile devices – initially for POS payments, though now also for one-click checkout on mobile commerce. I'll dig into Apple Pay in more depth later in this chapter.

STAGED WALLETS

Wallet holders have options on how to add funds, which is also referred to as "onboarding" funds or the "pay-in" to the wallet. I'll use these terms interchangeably.

Most wallets will offer a few ways to add funds to be more user-friendly. This can be via bank transfer, with a card payment, or cash top-up. The user can then use these funds anywhere the wallet is accepted – this can mean as a form of payment at a merchant, for peer-to-peer payments within the wallet ecosystem, or with a single merchant or brand. This latter example is a closed-loop staged digital wallet (I know, a mouthful). Many cities' transportation payment methods are staged closed loop wallets – like the Clipper card in the San Francisco Bay Area. A rider tops up a balance and then can use it to pay across busses, metro, and train services.

One of my favorite examples of how to top-up a mobile wallet is Gojek in Indonesia. They're a "super" app that allows users of the wallet to add funds through cash top-up. Super apps are an ecosystem of apps that meet various consumer needs, and a payment system that works seamlessly across them. Think everything from food delivery, messaging, P2P, to gaming. With Gojek, a rider can opt to be paired with a driver who accepts cash; they then hand cash over to the driver, who confirms the receipt of funds in their wallet. Those funds can then be used online by the rider. While there are many fraud and money laundering considerations, you can't beat the convenience. Additionally, it's a great way for unbanked or under-banked individuals to participate in online economies. While Gojek is not the only super app that provides this cash-in funding, I believe Grab does as well, they're the first example of it that I was introduced to.

WHY OFFER WALLETS?

From the merchant perspective, why offer wallets? The first obvious reason is access to a broader pool of shoppers, especially those who only have a wallet as their way to pay online. Additionally, however, mobile wallets can provide a better checkout experience. One-click checkouts offered by many wallets help reduce friction and can improve conversion rates.

For example, the conversion rate many merchants see with Apple Pay is more than 95 percent and more than 90 percent on Google Pay. Key distinction: remember that conversion and authorization rates are two separate numbers. Conversion can be defined as how many shoppers, once filling their cart and beginning to checkout, actually complete the payment to the "Buy" button. The authorization rate takes those shoppers who press "Buy" and looks at how many of those transactions are approved by the payment provider – whether that is a card issuer or wallet platform.

Ever wonder why some apps may ask if you'd like to refund to credit? They're storing this value for you in a virtual wallet tied to your account. Merchants in turn avoid the cost of returning the transaction amount to your card, have expected revenue, and keep your business. They also save on payments fees when a consumer spends those funds in the future, and if the consumer never spends the amount, they can recognize it as breakage revenue in some scenarios. For the merchant, it's a win on all fronts.

EXAMPLES OF WALLETS

There are more wallets out there than I have pages in this book, but given their prevalence, I wanted to touch on a few examples.

PayPal

PayPal was a pioneer of digital wallets. Multiple books have been written on the company, so we'll keep our treatment brief here. Check out *PayPal Wars* if you want a more in-depth tale about the company.

PayPal was founded in 1998 by Peter Thiel and Max Levchin to provide low cost, effortless digital payments for shoppers and merchants. They started under a different name – Cofinity – to facilitate peer-to-peer payments on PDAs but given that the PDA market in the late 90s was relatively small, they pivoted to web. They were perfectly positioned to take off as online commerce began to boom in the early 2000s. Not many other companies were creating native digital payments solutions for the burgeoning ecommerce landscape. Interestingly, Levchin then went on to found BNPL giant Affirm.

A key factor in PayPal's rise was its partnership with eBay, a partnership that drove its user base to one million customers by 2000. Before PayPal, eBay transactions were completed over mailed checks. Yes. Read that again and realize how far this industry has come in two decades. PayPal was easy, secure, and confirmed instantly. They pioneered identity verification and dispute management resources for buyers and sellers – many of the aspects we take for granted today in an online payment method were novel solutions to new problems that PayPal faced.

In 2002, eBay acquired PayPal, further codifying their symbiotic relationship. In 2013, PayPal acquired Braintree, the payment gateway that included Venmo – the popular, U.S.-based, peer-to-peer payments app. In 2014, eBay and PayPal split into separate companies again, and in 2018, eBay announced that it would be moving their payment processing to Adyen – another payments platform.

But let's take a step back. What made PayPal special? One aspect is the user experience and ease of use – signing up for PayPal was simple. An individual would sign up with their email, confirm the account, then add a credit or debit card. They drove early growth with steep incentives – $20 if you opened an account and $20 if you referred a friend. Over time, and with its viral growth, those high incentives were dropped to $5. It's estimated that they spent $60 to $70 million on the referral program.[17]

Secondly, there weren't many alternatives at the dawn of ecommerce. It wasn't the first online payments solution, but PayPal hugely benefited from market timing combined with the eBay partnership to drive adoption.

Finally, the international scope and payouts ubiquity further drove adoption. PayPal is a truly global wallet. They let users withdraw in fifty-five currencies, hold balances in more than thirty-five currencies, and receive payments in more than one hundred currencies. Globalized consumer retail boomed alongside, and was enabled by, ecommerce. Sellers and shoppers don't need to be in the same country or grapple with cross-border wire transfers to pay one another. By acquiring the remittances platform

Xoom in 2015, PayPal made many cross-border P2P transactions, as well as global marketplace payouts, turnkey.

Wallets In China

The Chinese payments ecosystem is dominated by two behemoths – Alipay and WeChat. From a market level, the Chinese payments landscape leap-frogged past card-based payments and the global networks. Instead Alibaba and Tencent, with Alipay and WeChat Pay respectively, have created ecosystems where payments are a core feature. Wallets, QR codes, and trust are what underlie their methods. Both allow a user to keep payment credentials or funds in the app and transmit funds to individuals or businesses online or in-person. Both have a user top up funds, so they're "staged" digital wallets that hold funds for users. It's most common for users to load funds by linking a bank account.

A huge benefit of WeChat Pay and Alipay, and likely a reason for the meteoric adoption by issuers, is that the QR-code checkout disintermediates the need for payment terminals. It's an account-to-account transfer on the closed-loop platform. There is no processor sitting in the middle, WeChat Pay and Alipay are the processors.

> **QR CODES**
>
> QR – or *quick response* – codes are a square barcode that is scannable and contains data like a website link or account information. They were invented by Masahiro Hara in 1994 to track vehicle parts during the manufacturing process but did not have a multitude of applications at the time.

They can be easily scanned allowing a shopper to complete a payment with supported payment methods. Now there are many use cases beyond payments, such as at a restaurant to access a menu on your phone, which became popular during the Covid-19 pandemic.

While WeChat Pay and Alipay are rivals, they do have different segments. WeChat Pay, being an offshoot of the messaging app WeChat, is used heavily for peer-to-peer payments and interacting with brands on social media. Alipay, tied to Alibaba, is rooted in ecommerce and used more for that purpose.

Alipay vs. WeChat Pay: Number of Active Users (Millions)

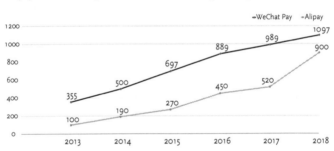

Source: Statista, Xinhua, China Plus, Tech in Asia

Alipay

Alipay is a staged digital wallet. Users store their debit or credit card details in the wallet to use for payments.

It was created by Alibaba in 2004 as an escrow system to stage payments between buyers and sellers on Taobao – the B2C platform of Alibaba, also the parent company of Tmall.

Its goal was to solve the marketplace trust issue between sellers and buyers. Alipay would hold a shopper's funds and only settle to the seller when the goods were received. In 2011, they introduced the QR code to enable offline transactions in stores. Because of its convenience and cost-effectiveness, Alipay attracted 200,000 offline partnering stores and 500,000 taxi partners. In 2016, Alipay's users hit 450 million, and 71 percent of the transactions occurred on mobile.[18]

Alipay is now the most widely used online and mobile payment provider in China, with a market share of more than 50 percent of all online transactions in China. It has more than 800 million MAUs and more than one billion Chinese citizens use it. It's been adopted in seventy-plus countries and over three million merchants globally. Signup is easy – all you need is a bank account and ID card.

Domination as the chosen in-store form of payment was also due to Alipay being much cheaper than traditional POS terminals – in the cost of processing a payment, but also in hardware, software, and maintenance costs that go alongside a "traditional" payment terminal setup.[19] Merchants are charged 0.55 percent transaction fee per transaction. Compare that to the 3 percent fees applied by card networks, and you see Alipay's appeal to merchants.[20]

Alipay uses QR codes for checkout in-store. There are two flows available: a shopper can present the merchant a QR code to scan, or the merchant can display a QR code for the shopper to scan.

Although Alipay was created for use only by Chinese citizens and residents with a Chinese bank account, the company did launch a ninety-day visitor's pass in 2019 to allow tourists to use the payment method.

WeChat

WeChat is the messaging super app created by Tencent – it's more than just a payments ecosystem, though that's what I'll focus on here. WeChat is used by Chinese citizens with Chinese bank accounts, users link their bank cards to fund the wallet, and merchants have "official accounts" to which they can receive consumer payments. WeChat has more than one billion daily active users, so it's no surprise that those network effects lend themselves to a powerful and ubiquitous payments tool as well.

In 2013, the account launched a way for users to pay things like phone bills or shop on Yixun – Tencent's ecommerce platform. In 2014, after acquiring ride hailing app Didi, WeChat launched functionality to order a car directly from within the WeChat app and receive discounts if you use WeChat Pay. This tactic was so successful that in Wuhan (population eleven million) they saw 60 percent of Didi users convert to WeChat Pay.[21]

The Chinese New Year provided a second successful growth hack, where family members traditionally give each other Hong Bao (red envelopes) with money inside to celebrate. In 2014, WeChat launched a digital option to send Hong Bao in the app. It required both sender and receiver to be signed up for WeChat Pay and catapulted the number of WeChat Pay users from thirty million to one hundred million.[22] By Chinese New Year in 2016, WeChat facilitated over 8 *billion* Hong Bao being sent, and 46 *billion* in 2017.[23]

Official accounts are blog-like profiles for brands that offer these businesses a platform and way to interact with potential customers. Shops can upload and manage items, be paid with WeChat Pay, and then ship to users.

In 2014, WeChat also launched a way for shoppers to pay in-store via QR code, and today it's ubiquitous and accepted everywhere from large chain retailers to street vendors. By the end of 2019, WeChat Pay was doing more than one billion commercial transactions a day across its 800 million monthly active users and 50 million merchants.

Apple Pay and Google Pay

Apple Pay and Google Pay are both started as device-specific wallets that allow a user to store payment credentials on their phone (or watch, browser, etc.). I'm going to focus on Apple Pay here.

In 2014, Apple wanted to support a way for a user to store their card details on their phone. They wanted cardholders to be able to pay over tap, using NFC (near-field communication) technology rather than having to carry around and swipe a physical piece of plastic. You already always have your phone on you, why should you need to carry around a physical wallet as well? The rise of Apple Pay has been slow; one key reason is that when it launched only around 10 percent of payment terminals had NFC capabilities. By 2019 only 6 percent of consumers would use Apple Pay at the POS terminal when they could, though it did displace Starbucks as the most popular mobile wallet by number of users in the U.S. in 2019.[24]

NFC

NFC stands for *near-field communication* and is the technology that supports contactless payments. It's a communication protocol that connects two electronic devices within 4 centimeters (1.5 inches) of each other to exchange data. The payment is communicated wirelessly, and the information and authentication happen without physical contact. Contactless payments are faster, provide a better customer experience, and can be more secure.

To support contactless payments in-store, a merchant must have terminals that support NFC. A shopper must either have an enabled card or a digital wallet that supports NFC payments, such as Apple Pay.

The Covid-19 pandemic accelerated consumer usage of contactless payments — in the first quarter of Q1 2020, Mastercard saw a 40 percent increase in contactless payments, and Germany saw usage jump from 35 percent to 50 percent.

Still, Apple Pay has a long way to go to be a key player in the U.S. payments ecosystem. A few key reasons slowing growth:

- NFC adoption, not disintermediating the payment terminal but actually relying on merchants to make an additional investment for NFC compatible terminals.
- While Alipay is about half the payment costs as card transactions, Apple Pay costs the same to the merchant as other card transactions. Additionally, it has a 0.15 percent revenue share with the networks and issuing banks, disincentivizing them from driving adoption.
- Although Apple has nearly half of the market share for mobile phones in the U.S. and 22 percent globally,[25] they don't have nearly the ubiquity of WeChat to drive the network effects that grew WeChat Pay so quickly.

One revolutionary aspect of Apple Pay was that it led to the creation of the **network token**. A network token is a sixteen-digit number that is provisioned, or created, by the network affiliated with a card. They are not the sixteen-digit PAN, are outside PCI scope, and in the past few years have shown exciting implications for increasing authorization rates and reducing ecommerce fraud. I'll talk more about that last aspect later. To start, though, let's consider the story of *why* a new type of authorization tool was needed.

We know Apple Pay allows a user to store their card on their iPhone (or wallet, or other iOS device). But this action has one obvious issue: the sixteen-digit PAN, or card number, as we learned about in section one, is a highly secure piece of data with high security standards for storing it – PCI. Yet your phone is not a PCI-secure environment. How do we then circle this square? Apple and Google got together to solve this with EMVCo, the consortium of card networks.

The solution that was created was called the DPAN, or device PAN. The DPAN is also referred to as a *network token* today. In short, a DPAN can be provisioned when a cardholder wants to add their card to the Apple Pay wallet. The affiliated network, say Visa, returns a DPAN to Apple, who can then store this in the wallet and also use it to initiate transactions. The DPAN has a 1:1 relation to a user's card and can be used to authorize a transaction. From the cardholder perspective there is no difference between a DPAN and PAN transaction. The classic PAN is often referred to as the FPAN when talking about network tokens or DPANs – this is the *funding* PAN.

Because the DPAN is outside of PCI scope by design, another security layer was needed. A cryptogram tied to the device that holds the DPAN is created to secure the transactions, and it's sent alongside the DPAN in a transaction. This allows the card's issuer to know that this DPAN is used properly. If there is a data leak and the DPAN is taken off of a phone, it's useless on its own to authorize a transaction. The cryptogram adds the necessary layer of security lost when downgrading the DPAN out of PCI scope.

The Rise of Network Tokenization

Fast forward a few years, and DPANs began to have utility outside of the hardware-based wallet example. These cloud tokens, now more commonly referred to as network tokens, are what enabled technologies like Apple Pay – now they're able to be used in ecommerce authorizations as well. The argument for a network token for online transactions is an increase in authorization rates and a reduction in fraud rates. Because network tokens can be provisioned at the merchant level, the card's Issuer sees which merchant is requesting a network token, and then has more confidence when that merchant authorizes that network token in the future. The cryptogram in this use case is dynamic and needs to be requested over API.

Why would a merchant want to request or store a network token? PANs work just fine, right? There are a few reasons.

First, being able to store shopper payment details without dealing with PCI compliance. We covered the concept of tokenization and PCI scope earlier – but merchants have only two options if they want to store customer credentials. They can invest in being PCI compliant to store the credentials themselves or contract with a third party or their payment provider to store those details. Network tokens allow a merchant to store these credentials themselves without the same level of security risk or ongoing operational and compliance investments. Because network tokens for ecommerce are created at merchant-level and use a dynamic cryptogram, a data breach leading to stolen network tokens is much less serious. It's unlikely that fraudsters will be able to use the DPANs, but when a PAN is compromised it can be used on any other merchant website.

Secondly, but relatedly, is the expected reduction in fraud across the industry thanks to the technology. With more merchants adopting network tokens, and acquirers supporting merchants authorizing network tokens, there are less opportunities for details to be hacked and used fraudulently. The assumption that follows is that with lower fraud rates overall, merchants across the board will see higher authorization rates and in the medium term higher authorization rates on network token transactions. The issuer knows that this network token is being used by the merchant who requested it, thus giving higher confidence to the issuer that it's a valid transaction that they should authorize.

Authorization rates should also see a boost because network tokens have account updater functionality "built in" – in short, the ability for a merchant to receive updated card details, like when a card expires, directly from the networks rather than reaching out to their customers. This has great benefits on authorization rates and conversion after an initial decline. Network tokens are interesting because if the underlying FPAN (the PAN a cardholder sees on the card in their physical wallet) expires, is lost, or stolen and then replaced, the network token actually does not change. The management of that update happens on the network side, and the merchant can continue to use and authorize with the network token.

Reduced PCI burden, lower fraud rates, and higher authorization rates are the long-term vision of network tokens, perhaps the dream even. Only time will tell if broad adoption globally leads us to that reality. Part of what that relies on is merchant adoption, but the more interesting aspect in my opinion is Issuer adoption. Each issuer must not only support the provisioning of network tokens but must authorize them and decide if or how to treat them differently than a classic PAN transaction. Issuer readiness varies widely from country to country, and with a very long tail of global issuers I'm curious to see how quickly adoption is at a crescendo point. A merchant can't reasonably reduce PCI exposure until every card in their vault has a corresponding network token – a chicken-and-egg scenario.

However, this asymmetry of issuer adoption is where the final, and more short-term, opportunity for network tokens comes from, from the merchant perspective. While some issuers are ready to provision and authorize network tokens, some of those issuers already *prefer* the network token. This means, all things being equal, a merchant may see a higher authorization rate using a network token. Because this is not true in every country or across every issuer, a merchant should take an optimized approach to deciding when to use the network token for uplift. While this is heavy lift, some processors offer optimization products. Additionally, for the uplift to work to build routing logic may be compelling for a merchant. An example of how this could look in reality is a merchant authorizing with the network token, but if that fails immediately retrying with the PAN to see if that can rescue the transaction.

I'm excited to see how this new tool for online card payments evolves with broader adoption on both issuer and merchant side. It's still in the early days.

mPesa

The final wallet example I'll illustrate is mPesa, from Kenya. It's also an example of "carrier billing." Created in 2007 by mobile network companies Safaricom and Vodafone, mPesa allows users to deposit, withdraw, transfer funds, and pay for goods and services with a mobile phone.

By 2012, there were seventeen million mPesa users in Kenya, almost 32 percent of the country's population. It has been key in providing financial services and easy money movement to the large unbanked population of the country. Users can add cash to their balances or make withdrawals in-person at various locations like gas stations and convenience stores. Balances can be sent using text messages and secured with a PIN – it doesn't rely on internet access, which has been a huge factor in its success, growth, and value.

CONCLUSION

There are dozens of mobile wallets globally. I offered a few examples, but any omissions aren't meant as slights. In Latin America Nequi, Mach, CoDi, Mercado Pago, and PicPay are popular wallets. In Africa, beyond M-Pesa,

Barter, MTN, Paga, ChipperCash, and are a few of the popular wallet methods to know. Innovation in the mobile wallet space is accelerating globally, what's popular today could easily be unseated next month so, as always, the best way to keep a finger on the pulse of what wallet is popular in a country is to be on the ground and speak to local shoppers.

CASH AND ATM TRANSACTIONS

Cash? For online transactions? What? Really? How?

Globally, 1.7 billion individuals don't have a bank account. There's a huge population for whom online banking is irrelevant, the major card networks may not be normative or present (not to mention, without a bank account or credit you are unlikely to be issued a card), and cash is still king. There are variations of payment methods that allow shoppers to buy online but finish the transaction with cash.

Many countries have cash-based payment methods that allow someone to pay cash on delivery or take cash to a specified location, like a convenience store or ATM, and use cash to complete the order. Cash-on-delivery (COD) methods accounted for 3.3 percent of online transactions globally in 2020, according to a Worldpay report. In the Middle East and Africa, cash on delivery was the second-leading payment method in 2020. For example, in Nigeria COD accounts for 23.2 percent of transactions. Using cash to complete an order placed online is also very popular in Latin America and Japan. In 2020, 5.4 percent of ecommerce spend in Latin America used cash to complete a sale, led by Boleto in Brazil. In Japan, paying with cash at a convenience store, called Konbini, accounted for 10.7 percent of online spending.

From a merchant-acceptance perspective, there are key considerations that exist when accepting cash methods. The first is the delay, which occurs on two fronts. First there's the delay when the transaction is completed by a customer, and they go to pay the amount agreed on. Then there's the delay in the time it takes for the system to settle a merchant. This is an important consideration for retail merchants who will be shipping physical goods. It's best practice to wait until the payment method confirms that the customer has paid the balance in full, thus completing the transaction. Norms around how many days an "offer" is open for varies by country and method, and some methods allow a merchant to pick the terms for when it may expire.

Another consideration for merchants is that refunds are not usually supported with cash transactions, as you may not know who the customer is beyond a name or email address. Not all methods support the reversal flow of funds – where the customer could go and collect funds they'd previously paid. This leaves merchants having to build workarounds like store credit, gift cards, or a transfer to the customer directly (that's a whole other can of worms).

BOLETO

Boleto is an extremely popular form of payment in Brazil. The shopper selects to pay with Boleto at the merchant checkout online, and a voucher is generated. This voucher can be printed, and the shopper can take it to a bank, ATM, or authorized shop that accepts Boleto payments. The customer can then use cash to complete the Boleto payment. Additionally, Boletos can be paid online by the shopper using online banking via their app.

Expiry: Merchants can choose how long the voucher is valid for; the norm is five days. For merchants selling physical goods, the time of expiry is a very important consideration, because those goods will need to be held until the Boleto is completed or expired. For these merchants, a shorter window may make more business sense. For digital goods merchants, where there is no opportunity cost loss by a longer voucher window, the default time may be fine.

Settlement: Once the shopper has completed the payment the merchant receives funds in two to three days. This is a key reason why merchants are keen to offer Boletos – the settlement delay for card payments in Brazil is thirty days. Additionally, Boletos are a fixed fee transaction so quite economical. Another reason is that one-third of the population of Brazil is unbanked – so a huge portion of the Brazilian population is empowered to make online purchases thanks to Boleto.

Many other countries have voucher cash-based payment methods - like Konbini in Japan and Oxxo in Mexico. The experience is very similar to Boleto; the customer generates a voucher and can pay at one of the thousands of locations that finalize payments.

CRYPTO AND DEFI — THE MIDDLEMAN IS NOW MATH

It would be obtuse to write a book on payments in 2022 and leave out the elephant in the room: crypto. There are many areas of crypto or "web3" that fascinate me. If you've enjoyed this book, you may love digging more deeply into elements of the movement, such as NFTs and DAOs. From a payments perspective, I'll stick to the core concepts of Crypto and DeFi (decentralized finance) that are helpful to understand.

Bitcoin is where our story starts. The Bitcoin White Paper was published on October 28, 2008, by someone (or a group of someones) using the name Satoshi Nakomoto. It proposed a novel approach to eliminate the need for middlemen in digital transactions. Bitcoin enabled peer-to-peer transactions online that could inherently be trusted. The transactions are all recorded on an immutable and cryptographically encrypted open ledger called the **blockchain**. The trust is built into the code, rather than a middleman like a card network, so blockchain transactions are often referred to as "trustless."

The blockchain is a network of computers, called nodes, who each share the information of transactions. Blockchains are designed to be decentralized, immutable, and transparent. Each node verifies the sender and confirms the existence of the amount they're transferring to another party. These transactions are synchronized across the network, creating a shared record of transactions validated by one system. If a single node is hacked or edited, this will be realized by the other nodes in the system. This prevents "double spending" –

a fraudulent user spending the same funds in two separate transactions. To further reduce fraud, each transaction on the blockchain is public and auditable. Many blockchains are also permissionless, or open, meaning anyone anywhere can participate.

Where fiat currency is created by a centralized authority, like a country's Central Bank, the creation of new bitcoin is decentralized and achieved through **mining**. Bitcoin is mined by computers who validate and record transactions through solving complicated math problems. Once enough transactions have been verified by mining computers, a new bitcoin is mined (created). A finite number of bitcoins will exist – twenty-one million to be precise – though not all of them have been mined yet. Mining is how new blocks are created; how new transactions are submitted to the block-chain for validation by the nodes. Currently, nearly 19 million bitcoins have been generated through mining. The "block reward" for mining and validating transactions is "halved" every 210,000 blocks, which is roughly every four years. Currently the reward is 6.25 BTC, the next halving is likely to occur in 2024.

Bitcoin is considered a *protocol.* In short, it's the set of rules for how each participant in a blockchain (node) should share data, process messages, and accept processed messages by other participants. Different protocols use different consensus mechanisms to validate a transaction, record them, and generate new tokens. Bitcoin uses a proof of work consensus mechanism, while some other blockchains use proof of stake. Proof of stake does not involve mining, but rather issues tokens based on how many existing tokens they contribute or "stake." I won't go into these concepts in more depth here but leave you to enjoy researching these aspects further.

Protocols essentially enable trustless transactions between parties. The community in the protocol verifies and records transactions based on the standards and rules defined by the protocol. Other protocols that are exciting from a payments perspective are Ethereum, Lightning, and Solana.

Custody is a key tenet of crypto – especially where value resides. Self-custody allows any token holder to "be their own bank" and is a strong selling point of crypto. This is when an individual, or entity, holds their own private keys to their wallet. All the data resides on the public blockchain, but the private keys which prove ownership of assets can be self-custodied. Self-custody, however, is not without risks. By holding your own private keys, you need to both keep them secure and not lose them. If you lose access to your private keys, you likely lose your crypto forever.

LIGHTNING NETWORK

The Lightning Network (LN) is what's known as a "layer 2" payment protocol – it's layered on top of existing crypto-currency protocols. The LN was designed to support fast transactions at lower costs than a typical bitcoin transaction and increasing scalability by supporting upwards of 65,000 TPS (transactions per second). It aims to solve the problem with a standard bitcoin blockchain transaction – speed and cost. A typical bitcoin transaction can take an hour (10 TPS), and given its high fees, it can render small transaction sizes impractical.

ETHEREUM

Ethereum was created in 2013 by Vitalik Buterin as a block-chain to support wider use cases than just P2P payments and to increase functionality. Ethereum today is an ecosystem of dApps, tokens, and other "layer 2" protocols. Ether (ETH) is the native cryptocurrency which fuels the network and is used to pay transactions fees. Ethereum is built to support more use cases than P2P transactions, unlike Bitcoin.

There has been massive growth over the past few years both in value of ETH but also the variety of projects being built on top of the network. In February 2021, there were $12 billion daily transactions on Ethereum.

Ethereum is programmable, meaning users can build a huge variety of systems on top of it. Today there are over 3,000 dapps (more below) on Ethereum, which has made the protocol synonymous with DeFi.

DEFINING SMART CONTRACTS

Smart contracts enable an ecosystem of Decentralized Finance, also called DeFi.

Smart contracts are, simply put, code that defines cause and effect. When the first part of the contract is completed, a secondary action follows. They facilitate, verify, and enforce an exchange with agreed-upon rules – allowing for a complex ecosystem of trustless decentralized interactions.

A smart contract is a program that executes an action automatically when the conditions are met – no third-party is needed to finalize the action. They are the rules of engagement for an agreement or deal, and the terms are ensured by code and transparency. In short, they do away with the need for a middleman for enforcement. They allow any type of exchange to happen with high trust between parties, whether that's a simple payment or other financial products like loans.

Nick Szabo, a researcher who works on digital contracts and currencies, is heralded as the inventor of smart contracts. He has a helpful example to better understand smart contracts: consider a digital vending machine; to get a snack, a user must put in the correct amount of money and select an item. This leads to that snack being dispensed. The same way a vending machine negates the need for a human taking cash in exchange for snacks, smart contracts act as this trusted middle party.

Ethereum is the most popular protocol for smart contracts, and the applications built on top of Ethereum using smart contracts are called "dapps" – decentralized apps. A dApp is a smart contract, or a set of smart contracts, with UI on top. You may be familiar with some, like the NFT marketplace OpenSea or the token exchange Uniswap.

DEFI IN MORE DEPTH

We've quickly defined decentralized finance, a term that's common to hear about in regard to cryptocurrency, but what does this really mean?

You can think of DeFi in relation to the four-party model of a card payment described earlier. To recap, all the parties needed to make a card payment (merchant, merchant acquirer, cardholder, issuing bank) are all connected through the networks. These networks are the *centralizing* function;

think of them as the consensus protocol. They make the rules, lay out many of the correlated fees and costs of payments, and act as conduit of data and funds. DeFi disintermediates the need for this centralized control – rather than a private company (though many networks are publicly traded companies), transactions are enabled and guaranteed by *smart contracts.*

DeFi enables anyone to access and participate in financial services due to its permissionless nature, regardless of where in the world they are. All you need is an internet connection. The common metric for the growth of the DeFi ecosystem is in "total value locked." This is the overall value of crypto assets deposited in a DeFi protocol. By September 2021, that number had reached $65 billion. As an illustrative example, take Compound, an automated algorithmic money market protocol. What does that mean? They let users earn interest and borrow assets against their crypto assets which they "lock" with Compound as collateral.

Another feature of DeFi, and crypto overall, is self-custody. An individual can be their own bank, and securely hold tokens and transact with them. There are also centralized exchanges, like Coinbase or Kraken, that hold a user's funds.

ON AND OFF RAMPS

These are how users can turn fiat in cryptocurrencies and then exchange cryptocurrencies back into fiat. This often happens through a bank transfer or debit card transaction, and there are many teams working on building efficient rails to help individuals seamlessly move funds between the traditional financial system and crypto.

For example, if an individual wants to buy a cryptocurrency using USD, they will need to use an exchange with on-ramps. Once they have a cryptocurrency, however, they can use various exchanges to swap it for a different cryptocurrency or use it for anything from P2P transactions, DeFi, buying NFTs, etc. These transactions are all recorded on the blockchain.

FEES

No middleman? Decentralized? So you mean that the networks and issuers don't take their cut? Sign me up!

Not so fast. While there is no individual entity setting the rules of engagement and related fees, fees do exist.

In the Ethereum network, fees are called "gas" – the amount of ETH that's paid to a node to process the transaction. Gas is paid by the user initiating a transaction to the miner who validates the transaction; this then incentivizes nodes to maintain the network. Gas fees on Ethereum are denominated in a unit called *gwei* which is equal to 0.000000001 ETH.

Fees are used to perform a transaction and document it across nodes on the blockchain. In today's world, gas fees can be high enough that they make interchange fees look cheap – especially for smaller transactions. More complex transactions require more gas, such as DeFi transactions on smart contracts. There are many projects that are working hard on solutions to high gas fees, but, as it stands, today there are very few scaled options for cheap, seamless payments.

BORDERLESS MONEY

Cryptocurrencies are borderless, which allow two individuals in different countries to securely and quickly send funds (or tokens). Blockchain technology and cryptocurrencies therefore pose interesting use cases for cross-border payments and remittances.

Moving money across borders is expensive, slow, and difficult. It can take three to four and cost upwards of 8 percent to send money internationally. This is in part due to the need for FX (foreign exchange) because the two parties use different currencies, and because globally banks are not all interoperable. We covered correspondent banking in a previous chapter, but moving money across borders is much easier, faster, and more transparent using crypto rails.

STABLECOINS

Stablecoins are digital currencies designed to have *stable* value – unlike many of the other tokens and cryptocurrencies, which can be speculative and volatile. Stablecoins are pegged to a fiat currency, basket of fiat currencies, or tangible commodities like gold. They are backed with reserves, also referred to as collateralization. Stablecoins can be backed by fiat, another cryptocurrency, commodities, or even have no-collateral and be backed by an algorithm and smart contracts. For example, USDC is backed 1:1 with USD reserves.

Stablecoins maintain their price stability through algorithms that can automatically rebalance the reserve assets. This price stability makes them more well suited for commerce, P2P, or as a stable store of value. While some call bitcoin "digital gold", stable coins like USDC can be used more freely for transacting. They act as a "happy medium," allowing holders to benefit from blockchain features like instant processing and security, while also benefiting from the non-volatile nature of many fiat currencies.

HOW A TRANSACTION WORKS

A *wallet* is used to store private keys, which prove ownership of your assets. It's important to never share your private key with anyone. You can then generate public keys that can be shared without risking the security of your assets. A wallet can be software, a piece of hardware for self-custody, or it can be kept on an exchange if they have custody of your funds. Think of this way: trusting an exchange with your private keys is similar to how you trust a bank with holding your cash.

Let's start with receiving crypto. To initiate a transaction, you share your public key, or sometimes a shortened version, called an *address*. Anyone can send a transaction to your public key, and then you use your private key to "unlock" the assets. Transactions then must be *signed* using your private key to validate that you own the public key. This handshake completes the transaction and proves you're now the owner of those funds.

Crypto transactions are always push transactions and irreversible: you share your public key, and the other party sends you assets. The same goes when you send a user crypto – they provide their public key or affiliated address, and you send funds to them. For this reason, it's extremely important to ensure that you're sending funds to the correct public key. There's no recourse if you send a transaction to the wrong address due to a typo!

EARLY DAYS

There's still a lot to solve with blockchain and crypto before they're ready to be truly mainstream payments solutions, but there is a lot of promise for future solutions. Beyond technology, there are huge recent investments in innovation – many are pouring time and effort into these problems and applications. There are more interesting uses for blockchain technology in tangential areas of payments, like identity and the storage/sharing of sensitive data.

Some aspects of "typical" payments that we take for granted have still not been solved for in crypto. There still needs to be progress in aspects like risk, disputes (like a chargeback), and fraud for payments to reach parity with fiat and existing network rails.

The global regulatory landscape for blockchain and cryptocurrency is nascent; it will be interesting to see how governments continue to embrace or hinder the adoption of cryptocurrency, especially for payments. Many regulators see crypto as a tool for criminal activity, like buying drugs on the dark web. It's important to understand that the U.S. dollar is the currency of choice for global money laundering, and over $1.5 trillion in cash is laundered every year according to the United Nations. This isn't to say more regulation isn't warranted, but blockchain technology can unlock new opportunities and shift global economic paradigms if regulators work productively with the ecosystem.

Section Three –
The Rules
and The Rule
Breakers

The best way to understand the regulatory landscape is from an expert, so we begin this section with a guest chapter contributed by Lithic.com and written by Matt Janiga. He's Lithic's General Counsel and Compliance Officer, Matt has more than a decade of experience in payments and FinTech and was an early legal team member at Square and Stripe. From there we will dive into some examples of local regulations and scheme (payment network) rules. We end this section covering risk: credit risk and fraud risk.

GET YOUR COMPASS, MAP YOUR BOUNDARIES

When you want to receive, touch, hold, split and transfer money, you are going to run into regulation. Regulation can often seem scary, due both to the jargon involved and the mysticism with which some gatekeepers and practitioners paint over the space. But at the end of the day, regulations are boundaries by which we abide. Once you understand the principles behind these boundaries, patterns start to emerge, and things become less complicated. So grab your compass and read on to learn how to navigate regulation in payments.

Payments regulation generally breaks down into four categories – safety, transparency, fairness, and policy preferences. Each of these categories has its own scale of sensitivities. Policy makers generally create controls that map to each sensitive area, with the intent of having the control mitigate a specific risk or further a specific desired outcome. Those controls are then communicated via various means.

This chapter breaks down the who (policymakers), the how (tools used by policymakers), and the what (key regulatory boundaries that set the map in payments).

WHO SETS THE BOUNDARIES?

Policymakers tend to live at the statutory or administrative agency levels. Some are elected. Some are appointed. Some are hired in at staff-level positions. Understanding which level holds what power can help your company and trade groups drive preferred outcomes.

Top-line policies for financial services regulation are set by statute. Statutes generally drive in one of two directions – they can create an administrative agency and endow it with supervisory and enforcement authorities – or they can set specific requirements for certain companies and individuals to follow.

In the United States, Congress or state legislatures have passed laws that create administrative agencies like the New York Department of Financial Services, or the Office of the Comptroller of the Currency ("OCC"). It's fairly rare for legislative bodies to create new agencies, as was done with the Securities Exchange Commission after the financial crash of 1929 or the Consumer Financial Protection Bureau after the financial crisis of 2008. Rather, legislators tend to reorganize existing regulators and update their authorities in response to actual or perceived risks to consumers.

Administrative agencies are the next set of policy makers, tasked with effectuating the statutory requirements and duties bestowed by legislators. The most powerful agencies hold broad licensing, supervisory, rulemaking, intelligence gathering, and enforcement powers. Examples include the Monetary Authority of Singapore ("MAS"), the United Kingdom's Financial Conduct Authority ("FCA"), and EU member state regulators like Germany's Federal Financial Supervisory Authority ("BaFin").

Administrative agencies can generally have a larger impact on your business, especially if you are a payments firm. Their three primary tools are regulation, guidance, and enforcement.

HIERARCHY OF ADMINISTRATIVE REGULATION

Regulation comes when a statute directs the administrative agency to gap fill the legislature's statutory framework. In the U.S., Congress's slide into a reality television show, with policymakers posturing for cameras, has coincided with increased delegation for administrative agencies to write rules to gap fill statutory holes. Legislators will sometimes set deadlines for rules to be finalized, but administrative agencies are often incapable or unwilling to comply. Other times, agencies ignore their statutorily provided powers. For example, ten years after the creation of the CFPB, the agency has yet to issue any of the open banking regulations that Congress statutorily empowered it to create.

Regulation often comes with its own rules about when and how requirements can be created, how much public notice must be given, and how agencies should respond to comments. In countries such as the U.S., regulations are also often challenged in court. As a result, administrative agencies sometimes resort to using guidance to further their policy goals.

Guidance usually carries the force of law, but without the administrative burdens described above. It also plays a critical role in gap filling and bending what would otherwise be plain language in formal rules. As an example, U.S. banking regulations would seem to create two flavors of prepaid cards – one offered directly by banks, and another offered by providers of prepaid access (often non-banks). Guidance that sits apart from the formal regulations on this topic adds a layer of nuance, describing where a bank is viewed to have a direct relationship with a prepaid cardholder. Merely looking to regulation may cause the bank and its FinTech partners to be out of compliance with some Know Your Customer ("KYC") requirements.

Guidance is also sometimes used to punish or foreshadow industry enforcement actions in lawful product areas that regulators disfavor. When the U.S. CFPB publicly fined Capital One in 2012 for credit card add-on products, it published guidance that created extrajudicial requirements for offering add-on credit card products like repayment insurance. These requirements were new; yet they were being applied retroactively to support lawsuits against the banks. The effect of these lawsuits and guidance was chilling, with most industry participants halting their sale of add on products. All despite these products being lawful under existing statute and regulation.

Enforcement tends to start where guidance ends. As in the credit card add-on product example, administrative regulators paired enforcement with guidance to drive a desired policy goal – the end of add on products. Readers in high-growth product areas like BNPL, crypto, and Web 3 would be wise to review Anti-Money Laundering and Sanctions guidance from agencies like FinCEN, OFAC, Her Majesty's Treasury, and AUSTRAC, as they inform how the agency is treating the most innovative products and companies in these spaces.

Not all regulation is punishing, and administrative agencies will also pair guidance with non-enforcement. Some regulators have formal sandbox or no-action request programs. The purpose of these is to allow industry participants to explain how a planned product meets policy goals, and therefore should be excused from statutory or rule-based requirements. Other regulators will engage with companies in private and grant non-enforcement requests on an ad hoc basis. These are generally not publicized, but experienced legal counsel will be aware of what a regulator is or is not waiving enforcement on at a given point in time. For example, the Monetary Authority of Singapore used to waive licensing requirements if your business was structured in a certain manner. But be careful about "breaking into jail" or closing off a product avenue – some regulators will say no, and others do not have the statutory authority to offer no-action or sandbox status. Again, this is where experienced payments and regulatory counsel can help.

KEY REGULATORY TOPICS THAT CREATE OPERATIONAL BOUNDARIES FOR YOUR BUSINESS

Safety

The brightest regulatory North Star is safety. Regulators want to make sure that payers and payees don't suffer financial losses, and that when something happens, the parties can be made whole. Regulators also want to make sure the government, and indirectly taxpayers, aren't stuck cleaning up wide-spread consumer losses. To further their goals of safety in payments, regulators generally resort to a waterfall of measures.

The first measure is chartering. In the United States and many other markets, payments have historically been dominated by banks, which are required to obtain and maintain charters from central financial regulators. Banks must generally disclose and propose their payment activities as part of their business plans, which regulators have the power to oversee and approve. Over the last decade, several countries have moved to create special payments charters. The United Kingdom and Europe are widely seen as first movers, thanks to the various Payment Services Directives that have been adopted in those markets. Regulators have gone on to create standards and regulations for firms that are payment services providers, as well as e-money issuers (what we would think of as prepaid or stored value providers in the U.S.). Singapore, Canada, and other large countries have since adopted similar frameworks.

The U.S. remains a bit of an outlier on chartering and licensing, due primarily to two reasons. The first is that financial services regulation in the U.S. is split and shared at the state and federal level. Since the U.S. Congress failed to adopt laws for payments companies, states filled the gaps with their money transmission licensing requirements. State regulators, represented by the Conference of State Banking Supervisors (CSBS) have done a good job lobbying against federal standards that might make state payment regulators obsolete.

The second reason the U.S. is a bit odd is industry capture. Over the years, various large industry payments players have been able to get state legislators to adopt carveouts for their businesses. It's tribalistically rumored, for example, that ADP has lobbied to successfully carve out payroll activities from state money transmission laws. And PayPal often successfully asserted that state money transmission laws did not apply to its business due to statutory references to brick-and-mortar locations. More recently non-bank payment processors have successfully won statutory exemptions in large states like California and Washington, and a patchwork of favorable interpretations and case law rulings on the "agent of payee" doctrine have largely helped payment processors fall outside of licensing requirements elsewhere. And several companies and law firms are currently working to identify and obtain clarity from state regulators where the payment processing exemptions apply to cryptocurrency activities.

If your company is required to obtain a charter or license, then you will generally need to adhere to capital requirements. In some cases, these requirements can be lowered or waived, so it makes sense to work with counsel to approach regulators when something is unworkable for your business.

Regulators will also impose corporate treasury requirements, such as requiring the segregation of customer funds from operating accounts and directing how customer funds can be held. One of the false industry beliefs is that payments companies can make money off "float" or interest earned while holding customer funds. While it is possible to structure your product terms to note that customers are not entitled to interest on their funds, it is hard to be a money services business and earn meaningful yield off those amounts. This is because states have strict rules about how customer funds can be invested. Even holding funds in money market accounts to clip a slightly higher yield can get you into trouble, as these funds often hold other instruments like corporate commercial paper (something not always permitted by state regulators). Due to this, most regulated companies keep customer funds in U.S. dollar fiat or U.S. Treasuries.

Transparency

Depending on which regulatory body you're interacting with, transparency into transactions might be equally as important as the safety concepts noted above. This is due to each sovereign nation's interests in gaining visibility into (and ultimately tracking and prosecuting) money laundering and terrorist financing. These concerns are largely embodied by anti-money laundering or AML requirements.

The key to understanding AML requirements is that they are largely centrally designed, and therefore similar across the developed world. This is because of the Financial Action Task Force or "FATF", which is a trans-national and intergovernmental organization founded in 1989 to set anti-money laundering standards. While FATF was originally incubated by the G7 developed countries, it has since been expanded to include a large swath of the developed world. FATF has standardized AML requirements through the creation of key principles that countries should follow to monitor for and prevent money laundering. Over the years, these principles have expanded to touch on best practices and considerations to curb terrorist financing.

The heart of the FATF, and really developed countries' AML regimes, is the principle that financial institutions should know their ("your") customer, which is often called "KYC." In payments, AML and KYC requirement generally boil down to collecting and verifying the (1) name, (2) date of birth, (3) address, and (4) government ID number of individuals. Regulatory requirements often contain a fair amount of flexibility and nuance on these points. For example, in the United States, you can collect a social security number, ITIN, passport number, or even a driver's license number, depending on what payment product you might be offering. Banks tend to have the most heightened standards but engaging with regulators will often illuminate quirks in the application of the law that allow banks and non-bank payments companies to offer magical product experiences.

Over the years, AML regimes have tended to move in slightly different directions. Europe, for example, has seemed to tighten its AML requirements for things like stored value wallets and electronic prepaid cards, lowering the thresholds at which a company – bank or non-bank – must collect and verify a card or wallet holder's personal information. The

U.S., on the other hand, has looked favorably as companies such as Square and Venmo used verification databases and partial identity matching to pair effortless customer onboarding with robust identity verification and fraud controls. U.S. regulators, whether FinCEN, the FDIC or OCC, have also invested heavily in understanding industry trends and how technology can better serve consumers, companies and governmental interests.

Another common requirement across developed countries is for financial monitoring and reporting. Most countries will require regulated entities to monitor for unusual transactions. Companies are then expected to investigate these transactions and report on those that are deemed suspicious. These suspicious activity alerts are centrally gathered by a country's AML regulator and related financial intelligence units. Data from these centralized efforts can then be searched and requested by the country's law enforcement agencies. In the U.S., this means both the FBI and your local police department could access a Suspicious Activity Report about things happening in your town.

Some companies look to gain scale in payments via partnerships, where a bank or money transmitter will absorb the regulatory overhead associated with transaction monitoring and reporting. While this is currently possible in smaller-scale partnerships, financial institutions will eventually require the non-regulated partner to take on some of the operational burden. This is why large payment facilitators have large transaction monitoring teams, and also "voluntarily" file suspicious activity reports.

Fairness

Fairness to customers, especially consumers and small businesses, is another key regulatory boundary. Generally, if you follow the front-page test (don't do anything you wouldn't want to read about on the front page of the Wall Street Journal), you'll largely be compliant with regulatory fairness requirements. However, some products have an additional set of technical requirements. You'll often find these in consumer products.

Technical fairness requirements tend to break along two lines. The first are disclosure related. United States consumer prepaid programs, for example, are supposed to disclose all fees and key product features like FDIC insurance prior to and during customer acquisition. The government, attempting to be helpful, has designed clunky tables fit for the Web 1.0 era that companies need to provide. Similarly, consumer credit card programs are also supposed to provide key tabular disclosures prior to acquiring a customer. And because we don't trust consumers as a policy matter, companies must provide similar tabular fee disclosures *after* a consumer opens a credit card account. State regulators are starting to require similar disclosures for small business credit products, showing an old dog can always lean on an old trick.

The other flavor of fairness requirements is operational in nature and requires companies to respond to consumer disputes. Building consumer dispute collection and resolution operations is time consuming, but necessary to ensure the company is properly complying with applicable law. Bank partners have generally gotten savvier in these spaces and will often translate these com-

143

pliance areas into tight SLAs related to phone support and customer service. For example, many banks sponsoring neobank card programs require them to pick up a certain percentage of customer calls within a small window of time. Others will mandate IVR systems to serve as a first line for customer inquiries.

Companies often overlook these fairness requirements for their customer service operations or understaff and underdevelop them. Product managers and engineers tend to receive accolades, staffing, and resources, while other areas like customer support are told to belt tighten and make do. But payments companies that take this approach do so at their own risk. United States regulators regularly track how many complaints they receive about a company's customer service practices, and some have even used complaints to launch intrusive inquiries and enforcement actions. Eventually, underdeveloped customer service practices catch up with you.

Policy Preferences

Every regulator has a set of policy preferences. These preferences are in addition to statutory duties, and regularly color how the regulator applies the law.

Sanctions is an example of a consistent policy preference. Payments companies are not supposed to engage with or facilitate transactions for sanctioned individuals. This is a legal obligation that comes from statutes passed by legislators. But regulators have wide discretion to adopt rules and exclusions around sanctions, and also add new individuals to the sanctions lists. These rules, exclusions and individuals are tinkered with due to political and executive preferences. For example, if national security advisors and high-ranking law enforcement officials from the DOJ and the FBI identify a specific individual that threatens the interests of the United States, they can look to add them to the sanctions list. This often happens with major drug traffickers, who unfortunately for payments companies also happen to have common Latino names.

Policy preferences can also be applied inconsistently, which has been the case in the U.S consumer financial protection and stable coin spaces.

In the consumer financial protection space, the U.S. policy landscape tends to shift depending on which political party controls the White House. Under Democrats, consumer financial services regulators took aggressive stances against credit card add on products, payday lending, neobanks, and BNPL providers. In some cases, regulators sued providers who were lawfully offering products, using policy arguments about consumer understanding and fairness in interest rates to bring claims against the companies. In other cases, the regulator buried companies in mountains of burdensome requests, requiring data analytics, product, and legal teams to decipher vague requests and respond on tight timelines. While consumers may have received benefits – some cursory and other material – from these actions, it was clear the aggressive engagement with the industry's largest and most boundary stretching companies was due to policy. In contrast, Republican leadership of the consumer financial services regulators saw more favorable industry rulings, even if they weren't always in the consumer's interest.

Facebook's attempt to launch a global stable coin network is another example of regulators using policy preferences to color the application of the law and ultimately shape outcomes. Facebook spent considerable resources and time developing a stablecoin system that addressed anti-money laundering and consumer protection concerns. Yet Congress expressed a clear dislike for Facebook's efforts and regulators soon followed suit. Per comments from the stablecoin's leadership group, the effort was set to launch several times, with regulators raising last-minute concerns and issues each time.

If you are going to build a global payments company, you are likely to run into unfavorable regulators ruling based on policy preferences. That's why it's important to have a great regulatory strategy and a strong policy team as you reach global scale and prominence.

COMPLIANCE

LOCAL REGULATIONS

As the last section illustrates, knowing the rules and regulations of each market you accept payments in is extremely important. Each country has its own ecosystem of regulations and governing principles that intersect with payments and money movement. It's important to know what rules apply in different regions, below I've outlined a few from the U.S. and Europe as illustrative examples.

Regulation Z came out of the 1968 Federal Truth in Lending Act. This regulation was created to require full and clear disclosure of terms and rates to protect borrowers. In 1988 it was further strengthened with the Fair Credit and Charge Card Disclosure Act.

Regulation E applies to the electronic transfer of funds in the U.S. between a financial institution and a consumer's account. It's the framework that implements the measures of the Electronic Funds Transfer Act, meant to protect consumers when they electronically transfer funds. For example, Reg E covers disputes for transactions at an ATM, direct deposits, or debit card transactions.

The Dodd-Frank Act was passed in 2010 in the wake of the financial crisis. The act is highly relevant financial reform legislation. As far as payments are concerned, the Durbin Amendment, which was passed as part of the Dodd-Frank Act, is particularly relevant. It regulated debit card interchange, created the Consumer Financial Protection Bureau (CFPB), and regulated network routing. Durbin gave the Fed the ability to determine debit and prepaid interchange rates. In 2011 it published Regulation II, which set debit interchange rates for "regulated" issuing banks – with more than $10 billion in assets. This means that large issuers were now regulated in how much interchange they can earn. Regulated issuers get $0.21 plus 5bps over the transaction value, but unregulated cards qualify for various other rates. It also required all debit cards to be dual-branded with two unaffiliated card networks, allowing merchants to choose which network to route a transaction over.

PSD2 in Europe, or Payment Services Directive 2, is a key piece of legislation requiring payment service providers to improve customer authentication processes and also to regulate third-party involvement. It covers many types of

PSP obligations and responsibilities: governance, open banking, SCA (strong customer authentication).

Notably it mandates that PSPs perform 2FA (2-factor authentication) on ecommerce transactions within specified scope:

- Both issuer and acquirer are in the EEA (European Economic Area)
- Transaction isn't merchant initiated
- Transaction isn't completed using an anonymous pre-paid card

2FA is defined as something the shopper knows (password), something they possess (one-time password, like a text), and something they are (like their fingerprint).

There are quite a few exemptions which allow a merchant to forego 2FA. For example:

- Transaction risk analysis (TRA): if the transaction is deemed low risk based on the average fraud levels of the merchant's acquirer or the issuer.
- Low value: transactions under €30 do not require SCA, but after five consecutive transactions *or* if the sum is over €100, SCA is mandatory. The card issuer can pick which to enforce.
- Whitelisting: a cardholder is able to whitelist specific trusted merchants to exempt their transactions with those merchants from SCA going forward.
- Secure corporate payments (SCP): transactions made through dedicated corporate processes initiated by businesses and not available to consumers.

SCHEME COMPLIANCE

Each payment method or card network also has their own rules. Sometimes they restrict processing from certain types of businesses, such as gambling merchants. And they often have rules around localization and other criteria.

The major card networks share a lot of similar rules. For one, to acquire card transactions locally, a merchant must have a local entity. However, not every non-card payment method has this stipulation. There are also rules about how to flag transactions and which data must be sent, to name a few.

Processing using a relevant MCC (merchant category code) is also a matter of scheme compliance. This helps issuers assess risk, networks understand traffic, and changes fees on transactions. While some merchants may qualify for a few various MCCs, many are quite clear. For example, airlines and gambling. Fun aside – dating apps use the same MCC as escort services (7273, if you're curious). Some MCCs are considered "high risk" – these tend to have higher fraud rates and chargebacks.

MIT AND CIT FRAMEWORKS

In 2018, Visa enforced a new framework to better identify "credential on file" or COF transactions, those that use stored credentials (tokenized card details) to process a transaction. This is known as the CIT/MIT framework.

CIT is cardholder-initiated transactions. MIT is merchant initiated. This allows networks and issuing banks better visibility. MIT transactions mean the merchant sent that transaction – an example being a subscription. CIT means the shopper chose a stored card to use for that payment, an example being one-click checkout.

Visa's rationale for the new data field was to provide better visibility to each stakeholder in the payment value chain to manage risk and fraud, which in turn should lend itself to higher authorization rates and a better experience for cardholders.

RISK

There are two types of risk in payments: credit risk and fraud risk.

There are also different types of credit risk – from the acquirer and from the issuer perspective. For credit cards, the issuer bears credit risk in the event that a cardholder may fail to repay their loan balance. For pull payments – think debit card, check, ACH debit – the bank may extend an overdraft and assume credit risk rather than letting the payment bounce.

For acquirers, they assume credit risk on behalf of merchants. If a merchant goes out of business or files for bankruptcy, the acquirer is financially liable for all chargebacks. An extreme example of this causing issues for an acquirer is in the event of an airline going under. Airline tickets are paid for months in advance. So when an airline goes out of business and is not able to provide the service, the customers will demand refunds or file a chargeback. If the airline does not exist or is filing for bankruptcy, they may be unable to fund the refunds, in these cases the acquiring bank must return those funds. For this reason, many acquirers not only audit the financial health of their merchants but will ask for a deposit they can hold to protect against this credit risk.

Fraud in ecommerce could fill multiple books. I'm no expert here but wanted to touch on it quickly. There are a few different types of fraud, with different meanings merchants, issuers, and shoppers. Furthermore, fraud is a balancing act – a certain amount of fraud is accepted as a cost of doing business. Zero fraud means you're blocking valid transactions and losing revenue. Fraud, then, is not just costly in terms of lost goods, but also missed revenue through "false positives" and the necessary investment into fraud teams, tools, and procedures.

There are many reasons why fraud matters and should be taken seriously. These include: 1) relationships with customers, 2) operational overhead, 3) loss of goods, 4) chargeback programs, 5) higher fraud can mean lower auth rates as issuers become less trusting of your traffic, 6) the rise of local regulations like AusPayNet and PSD2 to lower fraud rates

Fraud is a pain for everyone. Shoppers, issuers, merchants. J.P. Morgan's 2018 AFP Payments Fraud Survey showed that 78 percent of organizations were hit with payments fraud in 2017. As businesses grow, the threat of being a target for fraud grows, too. Many companies may think they need to ratchet down the transactions they allow, getting stricter with their fraud controls. This is too simplistic, and you run the risk of "false positives" and blocking legitimate shoppers. Research company Edgar Dunn & Company found that 24 percent of businesses reported that more than 10 percent of the transactions they rejected as fraudulent were actually legitimate customers.

Fraud from the merchant perspective is very much a game of nuance continually chasing the thin gray area where you allow enough fraud to not block good customers but blocking enough fraud to not get into trouble (revenue loss, scheme chargeback programs and related fines, auth rate impact due to Issuer mistrust, damage to brand reputation, etc.).

Effectively fighting fraudsters requires sophisticated, on-going analysis and real-time data. Trends and tactics change so merchants, acquirers, and issuers have to continually tune and retune their models and decisioning. It's a bit like whack-a-mole.

Fraud is expensive. If a transaction is deemed to be fraudulent in a card-present transaction, the issuer takes the financial hit (EMV transactions, or those where the cardholder inserts the chip, shift liability to issuers). There are times when the liability shifts back to the issuer for online transactions too – for example when additional authentication is performed like with 3DS. In a card-not-present transaction, the merchant is often left paying for that chargeback – and with physical goods it's a double hit because they've now lost the merchandise too.

WHEN CAN YOU CATCH FRAUD?

There are three points in the path of a payment where a transaction can be stopped due to suspected fraud.

First, on the merchant's side, before the transaction is even sent to their processor. Perhaps they're monitoring IPs, or known bad-actor customer profiles. Merchants also monitor cart contents – for example SKU-based rules if it looks like someone is buying a few items in every size, sometimes referred to as a "size run."

Second, by the merchants when they submit the payment and receive more data in the authorization response – like if the CVC or AVS does not match. These checks can only be performed by the issuing bank when the authorization is submitted. Depending on the response, however, a merchant may decide to cancel the transaction.

Lastly, the issuing bank can decline a transaction. Some of the earlier examples, like insufficient balances and expired cards, account for some decline reasons. But there is also "blocked card" and the "do not honor" response, which can sometimes just mean the transaction tripped the issuer's own fraud system and is being declined. It's the issuer's responsibility to protect their cardholders – so they're the last line of defense if a card may be being used inappropriately. To merchants and acquirers this can feel like a black box – issuers continually change their rules, don't all send refusal reasons consistently or with the correct label, and can have "false positives," just as a merchant can when they choose to decline a transaction.

Issuers want to protect against fraud for a few reasons. The first is obvious – to act in the best interest of their customer, the cardholder. A dispute, or chargeback, is not just costly from the perspective of the transaction value but also in the process involved in pursuing the dispute, paying customer service representatives for their time, etc. Operationally, the expense can be more than that of the transaction alone.

Conversely, if an issuer is too strict on fraud and declines too many "good" transactions, cardholders will get frustrated. If this becomes a continual headache, a cardholder may take their business to another Issuer altogether. Famously, in an effort for faster checkout, Amazon does not send CVC with authorizations. However, some issuers will decline these transactions flat out. CVC is a great way to ensure that the shopper is present with the physical card (remember, CVC codes can't be stored under PCI rules), rather than shopping online with a stolen PAN. From the issuer's perspective, a shopper-initiated payment without CVC looks riskier. In this example, issuers tend to bend to the will of Amazon; cardholders have brand loyalty, and you can't beat Prime deals.

Let's cover three types of fraud in more depth: friendly fraud, account takeover (ATO), fraudy fraud.

Friendly fraud are instances where the shopper does not dispute that they initiated the transaction but have an issue with the quality or completeness of a good or service. This could be a fake merchant who never had real goods, and thus none ever arrived. Or perhaps the goods arrived broken, but the merchant did not work to remedy the situation. In these instances, the shopper can contact their Issuing bank to initiate a chargeback.

Account Takeover is quite straightforward (as far as payments are concerned). Rather than payment credentials being stolen and improperly used, a valid customer account that has stored payment credentials is hacked into (or accessed), and a payment is initiated from that account by a bad actor.

Actual fraud, or what I call "fraudy fraud" is just that – the actual bad actors. Congratulations on catching one! These could be someone using a stolen credit card they swiped from a purse or bought the details of online. It could be an individual or a sophisticated operation shipping stolen goods to warehouses.

Section Four – Business Models

In an effort to apply what you've learned in the past chapters, I'm now going to outline three key business models where payments play an integral role: subscriptions, marketplaces, and B2B.

SUBSCRIPTIONS ARE EATING THE WORLD

Gone are the days when a subscription was just for a newspaper or magazine. Now you can get your toothbrush replacement, probiotics, wine-of-the-month, and work wardrobes as subscriptions. And this makes a lot of sense: recurring business models lead to customer lifetime values that are six times that of single-purchase models.

For merchants who want to offer a subscription, there's a lot to think about. How often will customers be billed? What will they be charged? What's the price of the subscription? How will cancellations work? Pro tip on cancellations: make it easy.

In this section I cover some of the payments-related considerations for a subscription business. Pricing and cadence are business decisions, and another topic for another day.

But once you have users signed up, how do you bill them correctly every month? How do you collect on lapsed or failed payments? These are the topics I explore here.

The best subscription service is one where the customer forgets they're paying for it; they're seamlessly billed each cycle, and they can keep enjoying the service. The last thing you want is for payments to be a point of friction for a customer when they're signing up for your subscription service. We'll cover three key areas that are core to a subscription's payments operation: automated billing, preventing declines for recurring payments, and rescuing declines when they happen.

AUTOMATE BILLING

If you have a subscription product, how do you bill your customers? For ease of explanation, let's say you have a monthly bagel service. You know Californians complain about the sub-par bagel offering, so you ship bagels from New York on a monthly basis to your customers, across the U.S.

To start, a merchant may try to manage the monthly billing cycle in-house: either billing monthly on the day a user signed up, or on an agreed schedule when you bill all or most of your customers. Sometimes this all starts on a spreadsheet. But pretty quickly that will become unmanageable; once you have dozens, hundreds, or more hungry bagel lovers as subscribers, you need a more robust system. So you have the next option: automate charging your customers with a billing engine.

Now you're faced with two options: build it or buy it. Building a recurring billing engine is no small feat, evidenced by the multiple companies who offer this service stand-alone like Zuora, Chargebee, or Recurly. For the big subscription merchants, owning the recurring billing engine makes sense. They've got the resources, want to cut out the costs of that provider, and may have unique enough use cases that they need a more bespoke offering than a vendor can offer. For most merchants, however, buying is the best move. Building this robust internal tool diverts resources from the core business. What you give up in margin and flexibility by using a third-party you make up for by being able to focus your energies where they matter: sourcing and delivering the best bagels.

Automated billing means more than "charge X customer Y on the first of every month." A sophisticated billing system gives merchants the ability to have multiple subscription tiers, offer different pricing, programmatically offer free trials and seamlessly convert to subscriptions, and even run A/B tests to optimize subscription pricing. Many billing engines will also automate collections for merchants – meaning retry failed payments to rescue that billing cycle. More on that later. The point here is that automated billing very quickly scales in complexity with a merchant's growth. For many, outsourcing to a provider makes the most sense.

LIFECYCLE MANAGEMENT AND CHURN

Churn is a key concern for subscription business models. How do you ensure that your customers stay, month to month? Those that leave are considered "churned." There are two types of churn: voluntary and involuntary.

Voluntary churn means a customer has decided to cancel their subscription. Don't let payments be the "positive friction" that allows you to maintain customers. To retain customers, you should really focus on the product and customer support. But if a customer decides to cancel, make it as clear and easy as possible. An easy-to-find button to cancel on your website or in their customer portal is the best path.

You can still incentivize them to stay with discounts or deals and optimize the cancellation flow to try and collect data on why that customer is leaving, but canceling should always be easy. This feels counterintuitive to some – why make it *easy* to cancel? The payments related reason is chargebacks. If you make it difficult to cancel the service, you run the risk of a customer getting fed up trying to figure it out or waiting on hold with a customer service rep and instead canceling their card or calling their issuing bank to initiate a chargeback. Chargebacks are expensive even if you end up winning the dispute, if they become too common merchants can end up in the networks' chargeback programs, which can lead to fines.

It's unfortunate that churn is inevitable, especially with how expensive it can be to acquire customers. That's why it's important to reduce *involuntary* churn. **Involuntary churn** is when a subscription loses subscribers who did not actively opt-out. While this is the more frustrating type of churn, it is also more actionable from a payments perspective.

While your customers may be loyal, their cards will expire, get lost, be replaced, etc. When you have a business where you store your customers' payment credentials – for one-click checkout or subscriptions – managing the lifecycle of these payment details is key. We talked about tokenization earlier in the book – securely storing payment credentials.

But what about keeping those credentials up to date? That's called "lifecycle management."

There are a few different products a merchant can use for lifecycle management. The most popular and useful being the Account Updater products offered by the card networks. Mastercard's product is called ABU, Automatic Billing Updater. Visa's is called Account Updater, VAU, and American Express' service is called Card Refresher. These services can have a huge impact for merchants – Mastercard reports that 33 percent of card-not-present declines could be rescued with the use of ABU.

Account Updater allows a merchant to get updated card details from the card networks rather than having to reach out to cardholders directly. I don't know about you, but I have never proactively updated my card details with a merchant. I wait until I get an email or notice from a merchant, then decide if it's worth re-upping the service. Sometimes I may also forget to go in and update the card even after being emailed. Clearly that's not the best scenario from a merchant's perspective. Additionally, prompting a user to update their own expired details only happens after there's already been an initial decline in that billing cycle. Account Updater allows merchants to proactively get card updates from the Networks to avoid that initial decline altogether.

There are two flavors of account updater: batch and real-time. Batch account updater is a batch file process where a merchant creates a file with each card they want to perform an update for and send it to their processor or gateway, or a partner who is connected to the networks for these services. If the merchant is PCI compliant, this batch file may have the sixteen-digit PANs; otherwise they may send a batch file of token IDs to their provider, who then sends the file out to the networks with the PANs. Each network has their own batch process that takes a few days to return the file with updates. Updates are sent back for each credential, or card, that has new details. For example, this can be an updated expiry. The merchant can then use those up-to-date card details in the next billing attempt, thus reducing the declines due to lifecycle issues and reducing involuntary churn.

The merchant can choose which cards to include in the batch file, the least-effort but also least-efficient is to send every card that will be billed in the next cycle out for an update. However, because each update comes with a fee it's worth the effort for many merchants to build some logic into which credentials to include in the batch file. An easy example is taking a look to see what cards in their token vault have expiry dates that have already passed – since these cards have already expired it makes sense to go out to the networks for an update. If a merchant has a very cyclical billing cycle – all customers on the first of the month, for instance – building out a robust batch process could solve enough of the lifecycle management pain points.

Most merchants bill customers throughout the month, so should they run batch processes weekly? What happens if a cardholder loses their card between the date the batch of updates is requested and the date the merchant goes to charge the card? This time inconsistency issue can be a pain point for many merchants – real-time account updater is a great solution in those cases.

Visa and MasterCard have built an additional account updater product that lets a merchant query for an update in real time. Visa's real time service is available in the authorization request and Mastercard has a standalone ABU API which allows a merchant to check an individual card for a potential update in real time. For Visa's solution, a merchant can include the VAU indicator in the authorization. Visa then checks in real time if there is an update for the credentials being used in that transaction. If there are then Visa swaps in the new, up to date details and processes the authorization. Both services are a great alternative to batch, by both ensuring a merchant receives truly the most up-to-date card details, and also ensuring that they're only paying for updates when they need them.

Important note: as of today, the real time account updater services do not have the same global coverage as Batch account updater. Mastercard is fully supported globally for both, where issuers participate. For Visa, only the U.S. has ubiquitous coverage with real-time account updater, so for global coverage a merchant would be wise to still use the batch product as well.

RETRIES

Even with great lifecycle management, declines will occur. How a merchant proceeds with treating these declines is more of an art than a science, but in this section, I'll give you some high-level things to be sure to consider.

Remember that the golden rule of recurring revenue is that payments should be out of sight, out of mind. When a payment fails there are a few options:

1. Ignore it. Let that customer churn, and focus on acquiring new customers. I doubt many merchants are keen on this approach, especially if you've invested heavily to acquire customers. It may be worth more effort to

reduce involuntary churn – trying to keep customers comes with a cost too, so merchants should decide if they want to take on that cost.

2. Reach out to the customer directly, maybe with an automated email that their payment failed. Some merchants will have a grace period, especially for digital goods products like streaming services, where the customer can still enjoy uninterrupted service. You may even do additional messaging. The problem here is that some customers may forget to take action, never see the note, or even worse decide to opt-out of the service. You're giving them the chance to reflect and asking them to put in effort to continue the subscription. You're giving them the reminder to decide if they still want your service. It's best to exhaust a few more options before this tactic.

3. Let's make contacting customers directly the last resort. The optimal way to proceed with declines is to devise a payments strategy to retry payments, intelligently, to reduce the number of involuntary churned users.

Option one is the best action if there was a hard decline. I touched on this back in the declines section in the cards chapter but will reiterate the point. Declines can be split into hard and soft declines. Hard declines, like a fraud response or closed account, typically mean that no number of retries will lead to an authorization on that card. Soft declines, however, can be successfully re-authorized. Examples of soft declines are insufficient declines, expired cards, or the annoyingly opaque "Do Not Honor" response. The next section only applies to these soft declines.

It's important to understand that each retry incurs fees with a payment provider – processing fees and some scheme fees. This means while more retries may rescue more transactions there is an inflection point where a merchant may be spending too much on those final few declined transactions. Add to that that there are diminishing returns with retries – a large number of failed transactions may be rescued in the first few attempts, but there can be steep drop off after that. To get closer to a 100 percent rescue rate the investment to rescue those transactions goes up. More investment in retry strategies, machine learning, A/B testing, sending transactions to a redundant payment partner. For some merchants investing to get as close as possible to that 100 percent rescue rate is worth it, it's important for each merchant to decide what's best for their business.

Collections, or the rebilling attempts after an initial decline, is about two things: time to collect and amount collected. I'll break both of these down.

TIME TO COLLECT

The longer it takes to collect a payment after that first refusal, the more questions and business decisions a merchant has to make. With digital goods, like a streaming service, grace periods may make sense. There are minimal variable costs associated with letting a user listen to another album, for instance. For a merchant who sells physical goods, like a subscription box that needs to be mailed, the window to get a successful authorization is shortened. Is it worth shipping the goods on faith that a retry will be successful? Is it worth the operational hassle if they pay successfully a week later and your fulfillment teams have to send a one-off?

At scale, a few days or a week in delay for a payment authorization could cause a cash-flow issue. Each authorization attempt also carries a cost – processing fees and any other related payment fees. So should you retry five times in five days? Consider how much that might cost. The card networks also have rules around what they call "excessive retries" – they don't want a merchant spamming authorization attempts to recover a charge. Visa prohibits more than fifteen attempts on the same transaction in a thirty-day period, which sounds low to some merchants and high to others. Some merchants will initiate a retry a few times a day; others will only retry once. There's a sweet spot between the two that merchants should aim for.

There's also a need to intelligently choose *when* to initiate a retry. This should be guided by the refusal reason – not all refusal reasons are created equal, nor should a merchant's actions be uniform across decline reasons. For "do not honor" an immediate retry may be successful, but for an insufficient funds (NSF) decline you're unlikely to see an approval. This should be obvious – for that charge to be successful, the cardholder's balance will need to change.

To rescue NSF declines, a merchant needs to think about when a cardholder may have a balance increase – pay days are the easiest and most common event to consider. In the U.S. individuals are typically paid twice monthly; in Europe it's once a month. There's further nuances around which days are paydays – is it the 25th of the month, the 15th of the month? Trying to understand where your customers are and when they may get a top-up of funds in their account is important to understanding when you should retry NSF declines.

As mentioned above, reaching out to customers is costly both operationally and forces a customer to opt back in when they may otherwise have passively continued using the service and being billed. **It's an art, not a science.** But each merchant needs to decide for themselves how many attempts or days they're comfortable with solutions that don't impact the customer, and how much they can invest in intelligent retry strategies.

AMOUNT COLLECTED

The other facet to retries is how much a merchant is able to collect with those retries – the amount collected. This means for one hundred transactions that decline, how many of those is a merchant able to rescue. How can a merchant focus on maximizing this number?

Depending on a merchant's business model, customer base, average transaction value, and decline reasons, the priorities and tactics may be different. For example, for merchants who offer both yearly and monthly subscriptions, it's likely worth more retries on the yearly charge declines. Converting one of those to a successful authorization is worth twelve of the other, though the value of the customer is equal. The monthly billed customer could be given a grace period and then reached out to if payments continue to fail, for example.

One advanced tactic is partial collections – billing for a partial amount. For some businesses and commercial models maybe *some* of the billed amount is better than none and a churned customer.

For certain services, like utilities, or certain business models where you decide that partial funds and trying again next month is worth more than customer contact or churn, a merchant can attempt to recoup partial payment.

There are two ways to go about this: one is an ad hoc attempt, "pick a number, any number" (though hopefully with some theory or data science behind the number). This could work. It could also raise alarm bells for your shopper when they see an unusual amount on their statement, leading to inquiries, possible chargebacks, etc. Clearly this is not an ideal nor necessarily scalable solution.

The second option is more of an expert move – a partial authorization call. This is dependent on a payment provider supporting this in their integration to the networks, but it's where a merchant makes an authorization request with a flag for partial authorization. The network for that card will reply with the available balance and an authorization for that amount, allowing a merchant to then make a capture request for what the shopper has available. MasterCard and Visa both support this with debit cards; an obvious use case is to allow cardholders to clear out prepaid card balances.

From the merchant perspective, the merchant can then request an additional form of payment for the remainder of the transaction value – but at least in the interim has partial payment. A common merchant type that uses this functionality is gas stations at the fuel pump. The pump is able to authorize the card, know the available balance, and shut off the pump when the amount reaches the customer's available (and pre-authorized) balance.

Partial authorizations should be treated like a business decision and may be a non-starter for many merchants. Your shopper either pays the full amount or nothing at all. But for merchants and use cases where partial payment is helpful, the partial authorization functionality can be a powerful tool.

The main takeaway is that subscription payments are a powerful tool that can be optimized to whatever degree a merchant has the appetite for. They can outsource to partners or build everything in house, treat every decline the same or build machine learning models to re-route declined payments. Some will perform two retries a day for a week and then email a customer; some will reach out right away. There's no "right" or "wrong" – so much of how a merchant manages subscription payments is unique to their product, billing cycles, maturity, resources, and customer base. There's huge variation in complexity, but at the end of the day remember: minimize the time to collect and maximize the number of transactions you save.

MARKETPLACES

Over the last two decades there's been a proliferation of marketplaces and platforms – they're great for discoverability and provide infrastructure (like payments) for sellers to reach those customers. From eBay to Zalando to Uber, Airbnb, and Shopify. Shoppers can view goods or services from multiple sellers, and many marketplaces allow a customer to purchase from multiple sellers in the same transaction. Sometimes they also offer quality assurance guarantees, or other shopper protections.

Much like subscriptions, marketplaces could be their own book. My hope for this section is to give you an introduction to key considerations, whether you're a seller on a marketplace, building a marketplace, or providing payment services to marketplace(s). Payments and the flow of funds in a marketplace are complex. A marketplace payment is more logistically complicated than a typical online payment, in fact.

There are four key parts of a marketplace payment:

- Pay-in: the shopper's payment for goods/services
- Splitting payments: the platform splitting a payment to allocate across sellers and their commission
- Pay-out: disbursement from the platform to sellers
- Seller onboarding: KYC, AML, and other screening to allow a seller to make money on the platform – and receive payouts

You start with a "classic" pay-in. These are the transactions we've focused on for most of this book. From there, that amount needs to be split – in two or more pieces between the third-party seller(s) and marketplace platform, who usually take a commission or fees. Alongside this payment, a ledger must track these balances at seller-level, and the marketplace needs a way to disburse, or pay-out, to these third-party sellers on their platform. For a $10 transaction the platform may take a 20 percent cut, so they add $8 to the seller's balance. Add to that the regulatory and compliance aspects of holding third-party funds: a need to KYC sellers, connect to payout partners, and comply with local regulations for transmitting funds, sanctions screening, and AML (anti-money laundering) measures.

Marketplaces don't only accept payments from customers, but also disburse revenue from sales to their third-party sellers. Payouts, however, aren't as straightforward as pay-ins. To payout a seller a merchant must first onboard that third-party, whether an individual or smaller company.

SELLER ONBOARDING

Depending on the marketplace, adding third parties will look slightly different. A car share platform may need to collect additional background details like driver's license to on-board a driver. A craft marketplace may just need simple information to add a seller. Crucial pieces of information vary per country and use case, but the governing principle tends to be "what information is needed to compliantly pay this seller"? These protocols are called KYC – know your customer. It's important to note that many of the aspects of seller onboarding are not dictated by payments compliance to take a payment, but rather local regulations or money services compliance.

Platforms that pay-out must be compliant with rules like anti-money laundering protocols and sanctions screening. I won't go in depth about what those look like, but information like identity, bank account details, and sometimes a form of state-issued ID to confirm are standard. The requirements for the amount of information a platform may need about a seller varies by geography, and in some countries different regulations apply depending on the amount the platform will pay out to that seller. For this reason robust onboarding and underwriting procedures are a core function of marketplaces.

To be able to process a payout to a seller the marketplace also needs to track all sales that included goods or services from that seller. This requires a strong core ledger that can keep track of seller balances when there are sales or refunds.

Within this architecture, a platform also needs to be able to *split* the pay-ins. Most marketplaces make a portion of the total sale to cover aspects like payments and as a service fee for the seller using the marketplace. In this instance, the pay-in needs to be split two ways: some to the marketplace, the rest into the seller's balance. A more complex example is if a customer purchases goods or services from multiple sellers in the same transaction. The marketplace then needs to split that amount over more balances.

AML

AML or anti-money laundering is a key concept when moving money. These procedures help catch and report suspicious activity. They ensure that the movement of funds isn't being used to obfuscate the origins of the funds or their intended purpose — like terrorist financing. For example, in the U.S., cash transactions over $10,000 must be reported to the IRS.

KYC AND KYB

KYC ("know your customer") or KYB ("know your business") refers to onboarding procedures to collect information. Individuals and entities are "KYC'd" for various reasons in the world of payments. Here are a few common times when a KYC check may have to be done:

- KYB of a merchant to be on-boarded to an acquirer, so they can start transacting
- KYC of a seller on a marketplace for them to receive a payout of funds
- KYC of a customer to either ensure that they are who they say they are, or to rule out that they are not an individual that a merchant doesn't want to transact with

PAYOUTS

Once a marketplace has on-boarded sellers, kept track of their balances in a ledger, and sellers have sold successfully on the platform, it's time to pay them out. There are multiple ways to pay out sellers – typically payouts are over bank transfers. But sellers can also be paid out to their debit card, issued a debit card by the marketplace that they can spend elsewhere, be mailed a check, settled to a balance on another wallet, or be given the option to use those funds on the marketplace itself as a buyer.

Bank transfers are covered in the above chapter, see page 79.

Push-to-card is an option that allows a party to push funds to a payee's debit card over the card network rails. Visa Direct and MasterCard Send are the products offered by the networks to support this but note that a merchant's payment partner must support this functionality.

Issuing a debit card to a seller is another more recent option, thanks to the advent of issuing startups that allow merchants to go live with an issuing program more quickly and easily. The reason a merchant may want this is two-fold. First, this is a revenue-generating option. The merchant, by acting as the issuer, gets to keep part of the interchange from every transaction when the seller uses the card. It may also be in line with their broader goals of offering financial products to their sellers. Some marketplaces and platforms have begun offering loans and savings accounts to their third-party providers. Secondly, it can allow sellers near-instant access to their earned funds.

Mailing a check is a low-cost option and may be preferred by some sellers as a way to receive their funds.

However, what a merchant saves in payout fee savings they will likely spend in operations to cut and track uncashed checks, lost mail, and other aspects of check processing.

Send to another wallet, cards and bank accounts are not the only store of funds for many globally – as explained in previous chapters. So a seller may want their funds sent to a wallet instead of a traditional bank account.

Settle to a closed loop balance or wallet is another option, some marketplaces may have a high propensity of sellers who are also buyers. In this scenario offering a way for them to use the earned funds on-marketplace can unlock payments savings for a merchant. Then they do not need to pay for the pay-out, nor will they incur payment fees for the later pay-in that uses that balance.

Each of these options come with additional workflows, but there are vendors who offer solutions for many. There are pros and cons of each, varying costs, and sellers may have preferences as well. It's likely that any marketplace will offer a few of these options, sometimes also due to geographic constraints if they have sellers in many counties.

The cadence of seller payouts is also up to the marketplace's discretion. Many marketplaces will hold funds for a period of time to cover potential returns or chargebacks and prefer to payout larger sums less often to save on the fees incurred to perform a payout. Sellers, however, typically will want funds as soon as a sale occurs. There's a balance from the marketplace perspective of risk, cost, and seller preferences. Some marketplaces have a portal where a seller can initiate a payout, some payout all available funds at a normal interval like once a month, others will payout when the balance hits a specified threshold.

Just as there is a vast ecosystem of payment providers for pay-ins, there is a large number of pay-out providers. These can help a merchant orchestrate payouts not just between types (bank transfer versus debit card) but also to cover the currency and cross-border complexities. Many marketplaces may have sellers in more countries than they have a presence or bank accounts in, so it's helpful to outsource the foreign exchange and local regulatory nuances to a dedicated vendor.

Regulatory Considerations

In many scenarios, the act of holding the sellers' funds is regulated. In the U.S., Money Transmission Licenses may need to be acquired in each of the fifty states to disburse funds to third-party sellers. In Europe, an E-money license is needed to hold seller funds.

There is a high barrier to entry for marketplaces, as compliance to hold seller funds is a huge investment in many countries. For this reason not all marketplaces choose to take custody of seller balances and be in the flow of funds. Some payment providers offer full-stack marketplace products, which allow the marketplace to outsource holding those funds. Two examples of this are Adyen for Platforms and Stripe Connect.

The networks also have rules around marketplaces. Visa treats marketplaces similarly to a Payment Facilitator, though with its own specific distinction. They consider any company who provides the platform or website to bring buyers and sellers together and also manages these payments to be a marketplace. So while many of us would consider a website like Craigslist to be a marketplace, Visa would not, as they are not in the flow of funds and providing payments infrastructure. Unlike a payment facilitator, Visa requires that marketplaces be in the flow of funds. They must receive and distribute seller/sub-merchant funds on their platform. Mastercard does not currently have a designation for marketplaces.

B2B PAYMENTS

B2B payments translate to business-to-business payments – that is, any payment made from one business to another. This broad category includes use cases such as automatic payouts, direct debits, accounts payables and receivables, and cash management. It crosses numerous industries, from marketplaces, to real estate, to crypto exchanges. Some of these concepts, like direct debit, were covered in the earlier chapter on bank payments – here we'll apply these concepts and go into more depth. This chapter lays out the breadth of B2B payments and how they differ from consumer payments in market size, payment methods, bank and payment processing requirements, and operations. This chapter was contributed by the team at Modern Treasury, true experts in B2B payments that are modernizing how companies operationalize money movement.

HOW B2B DIFFERS FROM CONSUMER PAYMENTS

Unlike consumer payments – that is C2B (consumer to business) or P2P (person to person) payments – B2B payments tend to have larger transaction sizes and volumes.

It's estimated that B2B payments already make up $127T of payment flows as of 2020, expected to hit $200T by 2028.[26] Last year, the global B2B payments market size was $870B, and is projected to reach almost $2T by 2028.[27] In contrast, the global P2P payments market was $1.9B in 2020.[28]

You might wonder why most of the innovation in payments is centered on consumers if the size of the B2B payments market is so much larger. While the late 2000s and 2010s saw the rise of contactless or NFC-enabled cards, mobile payment services like Zelle, and merchant terminals like Square, the B2B payments space went largely unchanged in the United States.

So why hasn't more innovation in B2B payment methods hasn't happened yet? A 2017 Fortune study identified the main barriers to payment innovation in this space as:

1. Inability to send remittance information easily,
2. Lack of proper process and historically underdeveloped systems,
3. Unsupportive regulatory framework.[29]

Among the largest regulatory challenges are the fact that the U.S. has many more banks than other countries and that the Federal Reserve does not have the authority to mandate new payment standards.[30] The latter can be contrasted with the European Union's adoption of the Euro, which enabled European banks to transition to electronic systems and standards.[31]

However, given the trends of more APIs and software being built to support the growth of fintech companies, as well as the global pressure to support cross-border payments, we're already seeing innovation in the B2B space accelerating.

PAYMENT METHODS

B2B payments typically take place over bank rails. In the United States, the most popular bank payment methods are ACH and wire transfers. Most countries have their own bank payment methods like BACS in the U.K., SEPA across the EU, and UPI in India.

Bank payment methods primarily differ based on transaction speed and availability. Payments over older rails like ACH and wire transfers take longer to settle and these networks pause operations on weekends and bank holidays. Many countries globally are beginning to modernize and digitize these systems. For example, efforts are underway in the U.S. to develop faster, 24-7 payment methods, starting with the Real Time Payments (RTP) network, which was launched in 2017 and FedNow, which is slated for launch in 2023 or 2024.

TRANSACTION SIZE, FREQUENCY, AND DIRECTION

B2B payments tend to be much bigger than consumer payments, both in volume and dollar amount. C2B payments are, more often than not, point-of-sale, single payments for goods or services; similarly, P2P payments are typically transactions between two parties. Consumer payments tend to be much smaller amounts and happen at a lower frequency. B2B payments, in contrast, often occur multiple times a day, both on a known cadence (e.g., a monthly payment to a vendor) and on an ad-hoc basis. C2B payments also focus primarily on payment acceptance, with money flowing in one direction from the consumer to the business (except for chargebacks and refunds). B2B payments on the other hand can involve both paying in and paying out in equal amounts, depending on the use case.

FUNCTIONAL REQUIREMENTS

B2B payments also have a myriad of functional requirements on either end of the transaction. Businesses, especially at an enterprise level, often have several systems like ERPs (Enterprise Resource Planning) and accounting software with bespoke workarounds or integrations to help them manage their (often mostly manual) payment operations process. The process can also be lengthy because of the number of administrative hoops it takes to process, settle, and reconcile a transaction – this includes departments such as billing, accounts payable, accounts receivable, accounting, and revenue recognition. Any updates or innovations can upset the well-established, albeit much slower, workflows, which may be the reason most businesses are resistant to changing their payment ops process.

WHY MOST B2B PAYMENTS OCCUR OVER BANK RAILS

B2B payments primarily take place over bank rails because they tend to have larger transaction sizes than C2B or P2P payments. Initiating a payment over ACH or wire transfers costs a flat fee per transaction as opposed to the percentage-based fees charged by the card networks. Also, since bank rails move money directly from one bank account to another, they provide businesses with faster access to cash.

BRIEF OVERVIEW OF MAJOR BANK
PAYMENT METHODS AROUND THE WORLD

ACH

ACH (Automated Clearing House) is a payment processing network that's used to send money electronically between banks in the United States. It allows for automated, electronic debiting and crediting of both checking and savings accounts. It's the most widely used electronic processing network for bank transfers in the U.S.

BACS

There's no single equivalent of ACH for the U.K.; however, a couple payment methods are similar. BACS (Bankers Automated Clearing Services) are bank transfers within the UK, including direct debits. Faster Payments is the RTP system in the U.K., and in Q1 2022 it processed £728 billion.

SEPA

SEPA (Single Euro Payments Area) payments makes it easy to send and receive cashless euro cross-border payments throughout the EU via direct debit and credit payments.

Wire Transfers

A wire transfer is an electronic payment made through a global network, allowing for fast, irreversible, foreign or domestic electronic money transfers. The system commonly used for international wires is SWIFT (Society for World

Interbank Transactions), a large network that allows banks and financial institutions to send and receive wire transfer instructions. United States domestic wires run through Fedwire, an electronic funds-transfer service run by the Federal Reserve Board, and CHIPS, Fedwire's private sector counterpart managed by The Clearing House.

RTP

Real-Time Payments, or RTP, is a payment processing network used to send money electronically between banks in the United States. Launched in 2017, it is the most recent U.S. payment rail. It transfers funds between two bank accounts instantaneously and is available 24-7, year-round.

Versions of Real-Time Payments have existed across the world in some way since the 1970s. Here is a short-list of countries with faster payment rails, from oldest to newest:

Year	Country	Name
1973	Japan	Zengin
1987	Switzerland	Swiss Interbank Clearing (SIC)
2001	South Korea	HOFINET
2002	Brazil	SITRAF
2004	Mexico	Sistema de pagos electronicos interbancarios (SPEI)
2006	South Africa	Real Time Clearing (RTC)
2008	Chile	Transferencias en Linea (TEF)
2008	United Kingdom	Faster Payments
2010	China	Internet Banking Payment System (IBPS)

Year	Country	Name
2010 (IMPS) 2016 (UPI)	India	Immediate Payment Service (IMPS) and Unified Payments Interface (UPI)
2011	Nigeria	NIBSS Instant Payment (NIP_)
2013	Turkey	Retail Payment System (RPS)
2014	Singapore	FAST
2017	Europe	SEPA Credit Transfer Instant Payments
2017	Kenya	PesaLink
2017	United States	Real-Time Payments (RTP)
2018	Australia	New Payments Platform (NPP)
2018	Hong Kong	Faster Payments System (FPS)
2018	Philippines	InstaPay

REVERSIBILITY

Card payments can be reversed. Credit card networks offer a guarantee of funds, presuming the cardholder has not yet reached their limit. However, for a variety of reasons, the cardholder, the receiving or initiating financial institution, or the merchant can cancel payment.

ACH transactions are requests for payment and can be rejected and reversed in a similar manner for a number of reasons, from a closed or frozen account to insufficient funding, to request for a stop payment.

Wire transfers and RTP are irrevocable once sent. This is why it's important to ensure all of the payment details and account information is correct before sending the payment request.

SETTLEMENT

Settlement refers to the event in a payment's lifecycle when funds are actually moved from one bank account to another. In the case of bank payments, settlement takes place directly between the sending and receiving banks; whereas in card payments, the card network intermediates funds settlement between the consumer and merchant.

In the U.S., card settlement typically takes between one to three days after the transaction is completed. Once the credit card network approves funding, assuming the card holder has not yet reached their card limit, the funding is guaranteed.

ACH can take between two to three business days to clear your bank account; although same-day ACH, if offered by your bank, can settle intra-day.

As long as domestic wire transfers requests are completed before the sending or receiving bank's cut-off time, they will be processed the same day, often within minutes of the payment request. Requests made after the cut-off will be processed the next business day. International wires can take up to two business days to process, as they are also subject to cut-off times, and have to be settled at both domestic and foreign banks, often running through intermediary correspondent banks.

Finally, as its name suggests, RTP payments clear and settle in real time.

PROCESSING

There are two types of payment processing: batch and real-time. Batch payment processing means sending many authorized transactions at the same time to respective banks for payment approval. This is often the case with merchants handling a lot of customer card payments. Real-time processing means the payment request and approval happen immediately, and the funds are cleared and settled.

Due to their near ubiquitous and high-volume use, ACH and Card payments tend to be processed in batches. Wire transfers and RTP payments are processed in real-time. Often this comes with a fee, but most RTP and wire payments are for large dollar amounts that make the fee seem reasonable.

OPERATIONAL ASPECTS OF MANAGING B2B PAYMENTS AT SCALE

While the capability of a business to be able to send and receive payments via multiple methods makes it easier to work with other merchants and businesses, it also comes with its own issues. As more payments are supported, the process becomes more complicated. Each payment method has its own time to settle, complicating reconciliation and cash-flow tracking at scale.

B2B payments also differ from C2B and P2P payments in another important way in that they need a lot of operations and processes in place to be managed effectively at scale. On top of just initiating and receiving payments, businesses also need payment controls to approve or reject payments, tools to track their status, and the ability to account for them appropriately. Since multiple people are generally involved in a business' payment operations, they also need tools to collaborate efficiently on these processes.

APPROVALS

Payment controls include approval rules, audit logs, automatic notifications, and roles-based access to streamline the operational aspects of managing payouts at scale. Approval rules let you flag payments based on criteria like amount, payee, payment method, and more, ensuring you have checks in place to catch potentially erroneous payments. Audit logs ensure you always know the source and reason for each payment, while roles-based access makes it easy to provide granular permission levels to different members of your payment operations team.

TRACKING

Flexible payment tracking capabilities include:
- Real-time status updates on payments you initiate and receive.
- The ability to automate payee onboarding by verifying bank account details and other key information.
- Idempotency to prevent the same payment from being accidentally made multiple times.

Another key aspect of tracking is settlement timelines, which are affected by how many participants there are in a transaction. The two distinctions are between a third-party *sender* and a third-party *service provider.* The key difference between the two is that a third-party sender intermediates the flow of funds, while a third-party service provider doesn't. Settlement times are always longer with third-party senders since funds need to transit through their bank account before they reach yours. They also have transaction limits and require you to comply with their KYC program. They are also generally more expensive, since they charge for the transaction risk involved in being in the flow of funds.

RECONCILIATION

Reconciliation is the process of verifying the completeness of a transaction through matching a company's balance sheet to their bank statement. You may have heard it called closing the books. Manually reconciling payments to transactions and cash balances on your bank statement can be time consuming and error-prone when you're operating at scale. It can also reduce visibility into cash flow. Make sure to pick a solution that can automate reconciling outgoing and incoming payments, as well as returns and reversals.

If you're doing a large number of ACH payments, you also need to think about returns and reversals. Unlike Wires or RTP, the ACH network allows transactions to be modified after completion. ACH Returns allow the party receiving a payment to send it back if they believe it was made incorrectly and are subject to well-defined rules. ACH Reversals allow the party making the payment to modify it after the fact – for example, if the payment is made for the wrong amount.

Supporting returns and reversals will complicate automating payouts at scale. If the payee's bank returns an ACH payment for any reason, you need to be able to track and reconcile the return to the original payment. If there's a mistake in a payout, you need to create a reversal and reconcile it to the original payment as well.

ACCOUNTING

Pre-built integrations with accounting software can simplify the accounting process if the software supports importing accounting classes and categories from your accounting system and tagging payments with them as they're reconciled. This can eliminate the need to manually export and tag data to your accounting system and drastically reduce the time it takes to close your books.

Conclusion

When I started in the payments industry, I wished for a book like this to break down the basics and introduce me to key concepts. I hope these pages have filled a similar need for you now and will accelerate your onboarding to understanding payments.

In this book we've covered how a payment is processed, the six payment methods in my taxonomy (cards, banking methods, wallets, cash-based methods, checks, and crypto), compliance and the role of regulations, and illustrated how payments are a core consideration for some business models – namely subscriptions, marketplaces, and B2B. We've defined dozens of terms for you to add to your payments vocabulary.

The industry is ever-changing due to innovation and regulation. Consumer behaviors change, economic forces shift, and banking norms evolve. Even so, the core concepts we've covered here should hold true for years to come.

I want to wrap this book by saying how excited I am to welcome you into the world of payments. I hope the chapters above have proved useful as you continue to learn more and can provide a strong foundation from which to further your payments knowledge.

Index

Acknowledgements

This book has been a year and a half in the making from the day I decided to get it out of my mind and onto paper. There are dozens of individuals who have been integral to my understanding of the global payment landscape, and many more who got me to a place where I could write an entire book.

Endless gratitude to my friends and family who supported me through this endeavor and only rarely suggested this should be a blog instead.

Special thanks to my many Adyen colleagues who equipped me with the knowledge that served as the basis for this book. During my tenure, there was no better place in the world of global payments to fall in love with the industry and get my sea legs.

I'd like to acknowledge the sponsors of this book: Modern Treasury and Lithic. Without them, this may not be in your hands today, and it would definitely not be as robust of a tome. They contributed valuable sections to this book. Thank you especially to Matt Janiga, Pranav Deshpande, and Chris Frakes.

To my group of subject matter expert editors, I'm grateful for your keen eye and kind judgement, as well as valuable additions to making this book comprehensive and correct: Ajay Moti, Bruno Faviero, Daniel Yubi, David Adams, Fred Potter, Jamshed Vesuna, Jillian Cohn, Lionel Tan, Nina Mohanty, and Raphael Shorser.

Thank you to my friends in the industry who fueled my endless curiosity by being generous with their time and experiences. And also to the people I tested material with, asked questions of, and clarified the content of the book with. Especially: Brianna Wolfson, Bryan Wank, Jennifer Dailey-Helgestad, Mithat Can, Ricky Tan, Sarah Hodges, and Thijs Niks.

Last, but certainly not least, I'd like to thank you for picking this book up and diving into the world of payments with me.

Author Bio

Sophia is a payments nerd and recent founder in the payments space. Previously, she worked across commercial and product teams at Adyen, also helping to train new hires and serving on the board of PaymentEd. She's fascinated by the physical mechanisms of the global economy and hopes to share her love and understanding of payments through this book.

She holds an MSc in International Political Economy from The London School of Economics and BA from Tufts University. Sophia lives in San Francisco, California with her dog, Earl.

References

1   "Covid-19 Isn't Canceling the Holiday Season – Press Release."
    Deloitte United States, October 22, 2020. https://www2.deloitte.
    com/us/en/pages/about-deloitte/articles/press-releases/delo
    itte-covid19-isnt-cancelling-the-holiday-season.html.

2   April Berthene. Nov 10, 2020. "What Retailers Need to Know about
    Gift Card Fraud." Digital Commerce 360. https://www.digital
    commerce360.com/article/gift-card-scams-fraud/#:~:text=
    An percent20 estimated percent20 10 percent2D 25 percent 25 percent
    20 of,as percent20 an percent20 online percent20 payment percent20
    method.

3   "Know Your Payments – Routing Basics." Know Your Payments."
    http://www.knowyourpayments.com/routing-basics/.

4   "J.P. Morgan North American Equity Research – Federal Reserve."
    https://www.federalreserve.gov/newsevents/rr-commpublic/
    visa_report_20101115.pdf.

5   Editors, eMarketer. "Ecommerce Continues Strong Gains amid
    Global Economic Uncertainty." Insider Intelligence. Insider Intelli-
    gence, June 30, 2019. https://www.emarketer.com/content/ecom
    merce-continues-strong-gains-amid-global-economic-uncertainty.

6   Fed. "Forrester Data: Online Cross-Border Retail Forecast, 2017
    to 2022 (Global)." Forrester. https://www.forrester.com/report/
    Forrester+Data+Online+CrossBorder+Retail+Forecast+
    2017+To+2022+Global/-/E-RES137898.

7   "The Global Payments Report 2021." Worldpay.globalpayments
    report.com. Accessed February 1, 2022. https://worldpay.global
    paymentsreport.com/en/.

8   Gutierrez, Maxnaun. "Why Pix Is the Revolution of Consumer Experience in Brazil." PaymentsJournal, February 24, 2021. https://www.paymentsjournal.com/why-pix-is-the-revolution-of-consumer-experience-in-brazil/.

9   PYMNTS.com. "6% Of People with Iphones Use Apple Pay in-Store." PYMNTS.com, September 7, 2021. https://www.pymnts.com/apple-pay-tracker/2021/7-years-later-6pct-people-with-iphones-in-us-use-apple-pay-in-store/.

10   "The Rise of Installment Selling." Buy now, pay later -- easy payments: The Rise of Installment Selling. Accessed February 11, 2022. https://www.library.hbs.edu/hc/credit/credit4b.html.

11   "Risky Business? Open Invoice Payments in Germany." ACI Worldwide, May 11, 2021. https://www.aciworldwide.com/blog/risky-business-open-invoice-payments-in-germany.

12   "The Payments Revolution." The Payments Revolution - Fintech Unwrapped 2.0. Sifted, n.d. https://content.sifted.eu/wp-content/uploads/2021/04/30185334/Sifted-Report-on-the-Payments-Revolution.pdf.

13   "Buy Now, Pay Later – Boom or Bust?" The Strawhecker Group, April 29, 2021. https://thestrawgroup.com/buy-now-pay-later-boom-or-bust/.

14   Ibid. "The Payments Revolution." Sifted.

15   Ibid. "The Payments Revolution." Sifted.

16   "How Old-Style Buy Now, Pay Later Became Trendy 'BNPL.'" Bloomberg.com. Bloomberg. https://www.bloomberg.com/news/articles/2021-09-15/how-old-style-buy-now-pay-later-became-trendy-bnpl-quicktake.

17   YouTube. YouTube, 2013. https://www.youtube.com/watch?v=vDwzmJpI4io&t=680s.

18   Chinanews. 中国新闻网. Accessed February 12, 2022. https://www.chinanews.com.cn/business/2017/01-05/8114117.shtml.

19   "A Hangzhou Story: The Development of China's Mobile ..." Accessed February 12, 2022. https://lkyspp.nus.edu.sg/docs/default-source/case-studies/a-hangzhou-story.pdf?sfvrsn=2bb6690a_2.

20   "Chinese Payment Systems Overview: AliPay." Sampi.co, June 23, 2021. https://sampi.co/alipay-payment/.

21 Rodenbaugh, Ryan. "WeChat: A Not so Brief History." East Meets West. East Meets West, July 19, 2020. https://eastmeetswest. substack.com/p/wechat-a-not-so-brief-history.

22 Carsten, Paul. "China's Tencent Celebrates Year of Horse with Mobile Gifts." Reuters. Thomson Reuters, January 29, 2014. https://www.reuters.com/article/us-tencent-chinesenewyear/chinas-tencent-celebrates-year-of-horse-with-mobile-gifts-idUSBREA0S0L120140129.

23 Horwitz, Josh. "Over 8 Billion 'Red Envelopes' Were Sent over WeChat during Chinese New Year." Quartz. Quartz. Accessed February 12, 2022. https://qz.com/613384/over-8-billion-red-envelopes-were-sent-over-wechat-during-chinese-new-year/.

24 PYMNTS.com. "6% Of People with Iphones Use Apple Pay in-Store." PYMNTS.com, September 7, 2021. https://www.pymnts.com/apple-pay-tracker/2021/7-years-later-6pct-people-with-iphones-in-us-use-apple-pay-in-store/.

25 Counterpoint. "Global Smartphone Market Share: By Quarter." Counterpoint Research, February 9, 2022. https://www.counterpointresearch.com/global-smartphone-share/.

26 B2B: How the next payments frontier will unleash small business. Equity Research, 2018. https://knowen-production.s3.amazonaws.com/uploads/attachment/file/3460/Global percent2BTechnology_ percent2BB2B_ percent2BHow percent2Bthe percent2Bnext percent2Bpayments percent2Bfrontier percent2Bwill percent2Bunleash percent2Bsmall percent2Bbusiness percent 2B.pdf

27 Global B2B Payments Market. Allied Market Research, 2020. https://www.alliedmarketresearch.com/b2b-payments-market-A08183

28 Zion Market Research, 2020. https://www.zionmarketresearch.com/report/p2p-payment-market

29 Fortune 1500 Study, 2017. https://go.nacha.org/crfsurveyresources

30 FRB: How does the US compare with foreign banking systems? https://www.frbsf.org/education/publications/doctor-econ/2002/april/us-banking-system-foreign/

31 Payment Systems in the Euro Area. https://www.bis.org/cpmi/paysys/ecbcomp.pdf

Made in the USA
Middletown, DE
19 November 2024

64982693R00117